THE GASLIGHTING & NARCISSISTIC ABUSE RECOVERY WORKBOOK

A 12-WEEK MASTER PLAN TO RECOGNIZE NARCISSISTS, AVOID THE GASLIGHTING EFFECT, EMBRACE WHO YOU ARE & BREAK FREE FROM EMOTIONAL AND NARCISSISTIC ABUSE

ANDREI NEDELCU

TABLE OF CONTENTS

INTRODUCTION

"I still struggle to understand whether I was in an abusive relationship or if it was just me being full of it. There were days... many, many days... when he made me feel like a second or third choice in his life. I know I was never his priority, but what makes it so confusing is that there were also days when I felt he was really good to me—those are the days I feel guilty over. Sometimes, I remember that we were good together, and then I walked away. Thinking about that makes me feel guilty. Mostly, I don't allow myself to think about those times, for it only confuses me more. It makes me doubt my choice to leave, and I wonder if I deserved better when I said I did. I don't want to question my choices. I want to know that I made the right choice to walk away. Most days, I know that I did, but there are also many days when I doubt myself as I wonder if my perceptions were all wrong. I'll never go back, but I want to be confident in what I've chosen for my life. It is hard, though, as, at one point, I picked him—was that a mistake, or am I the flawed one? The world is watching me to see if I'll make another mistake. It is a lot of pressure to deal with. He looked devastated, making me feel worse for choosing me. But even then, he didn't fight for me. Was it because I wasn't important enough? He let me go as if he had had enough and was ready to move on to someone else. He did. I doubt myself, and I hate that. Is it possible to be really mean to someone while being nice? Is it possible to suppress and uplift someone at the same time? It is so confusing. Why would you do that to someone you love? I sometimes wish he would've lifted his hand at me; it would've given me the certainty that he was wrong and I was right. He didn't. Now, I am left with this confusion keeping me from moving forward. I wish I knew for sure what I did wrong and how I should continue to become myself again."

Does Sam's story sound familiar? She came to see me about 3 years ago. She was desperate to move on with her life, as it was already 18 months since she walked out of a relationship with a narcissist. Yet, she was still doubting every choice, putting herself last, and battling persistent self-doubt and confusion that was sometimes overwhelming.

When living with a narcissist, gaslighting becomes your reality. It doesn't happen instantly, and the incidences of severe gaslighting may even come and go. So, for sure, there will be times when things are good. These are the moments when the narcissistic ego is in a state of confidence, and the damage they cause to others is minimized. While these times are limited—and as you are starving for recognition and attention—you'll grab these moments with both hands and cherish them far more than they were worth.

The only way Sam could set herself free to trust her decisions again and move on with her life was to learn how to manage her emotions, become confident in her choices, and live her life to the fullest. Sam just had a fantastic first six months of her business, a venture she would never have trusted herself to take on when she walked into my office. She is even dating someone again, and while it is not serious, she has learned so much from her past mistakes. Now, she is much more capable of distinguishing between whom she wants to make herself vulnerable to and let into her life and whom she would rather keep at a distance.

Before making any progress in your life, you need to identify your problem and the force you are up against. This makes recovering from life with a narcissist exceptionally hard. Gaslighting doesn't leave scars like physical abuse, not even emotional scars as a result of severe emotional or verbal abuse; instead, it robs you of your confidence, instills doubt in your mind, and, in that way, it has a debilitating effect on your life.

I want you to find your rhythm again, to get into motion enabling progress in your life. I want you to find yourself and become all you can be, much more than who you think you are now. I am guiding you, sharing trusted and tested techniques and questions you need to ponder to gain clarity.

Sam often said how lonely she felt and as if everyone was waiting for her to make a mess again. Recovery is, for many, an isolated place, loaded with unnecessary stress and tension to perform and excel. Can I reaffirm right now that you are not alone? You didn't make a mess. You did nothing wrong. No, if you stepped out of a relationship riddled with the narcissistic toxin, you are much stronger than what you give yourself credit for. Yet, I've also been in the psychologist chair long enough to know that strength means nothing if you don't acknowledge its presence inside you.

Are you ready to break free from self-doubt, employ courage in your abilities, and know you are strong enough to soar above the gripping hands of doubt that keep you grounded? Waiting for the right moment is futile; you are only elongating your suffering while life passes by.

Always remember that, regardless of whether you will step up and serve the highest version of yourself or remain a spectator on the sideline, time will pass anyway. Don't let time run out on you. Today is just as much of a great day to start the rest of your life. Are you ready to come with me on this journey of healing?

Week 1: Activity box

Write down your name and today's date. With patience and consideration, think about how you feel at this moment. If all the areas of your life were in order, what would your life look like?

WEEK 1

WHAT IS GASLIGHTING

Since the very start of Lilly and Mark's relationship, Lilly would be taking the backseat. Mark didn't like her family, so they hardly ever saw them. Mark didn't think much of her career, so he often demeaned her accomplishments. He considered his career far more important than Lilly's, even though she was much more qualified than him. Mark believed his career was more important because he earned more money than Lilly. Lilly earned less as she was busy getting her business off the ground while running the household, taking care of her son from a previous marriage, and being very involved in his school activities. Money meant power, and it was a way for Mark to establish control over Lilly. He would often expect her to do things just because he didn't have time to do it and would think nothing of passing his responsibilities onto her. Whenever she accomplished something, he would congratulate her but always end it with a patronizing comment or act. When Lilly published her first book, Mark would tell all his friends about what an excellent book it was and what a fantastic writer his wife was; he thrived on the admiration others would express. But, whenever Lilly asked him when he was planning to read her book—as she couldn't understand how he could say all these things about her book without reading a single sentence—Mark would shrug and state that there was no need for him to read it.

When Lilly attempted to address her concerns with Mark, he would give the impression that he didn't have time for another of her "emotional rantings," telling her she can capture all her grievances in bullet points, and he'll read it when he gets to it.

Neither Mark nor Lilly may realize it, but his narcissistic tendencies are pretty strong, and he is gaslighting Lilly, diminishing her self-worth, disregarding her feelings, and reducing her confidence. Mark and Lilly are in a romantic relationship, but gaslighting is also prevalent in parental relationships, friendships, and work.

Week 1: What is gaslighting?

From Lilly and Mark's example: what are the most worrying issues?

WHAT IS GASLIGHTING?

In 1938, the play *Angel Street* hit the stage, and shortly after, Alfred Hitchcock adapted the play into a film, *Gaslight*. The script contained the story of a man trying to convince his wife that she was going insane. His actions were driven by his intention to steal from her. From here, the term *gaslighting* was adopted to describe a type of psychological abuse that included attempts to instill confusion and self-doubt in another. Through this behavior, the gaslighter tries to control the other.

THE MOST COMMON GASLIGHTING TECHNIQUES

The foundation of gaslighting remains the same, but there are different techniques that the gaslighter can follow to achieve the desired outcome. Each of the following standard gaslighting methods is aimed at confusing another through behavior, encouraging them to question reality.

LYING

Gaslighters would often employ lying to achieve the desired outcome. They may blatantly try to deceive you, and they'll stick to their lies even when you catch them and confront them. Even if you present proof to them, indicating that you know they are lying, they'll remain true to their version, attempting to make you question your ability to determine what is reality. They'll even go as far as to accuse you of making up stories and say that certain events, that you recall, actually never happened, as if they are mere figments of your imagination.

DISCREDITING

While the gaslighter may come across as a caring individual concerned with your well-being, they may share stories about you behind your back, presenting you as a crazy person in your absence. Sadly, the typical outcome is that those who were supposed to support you wind up turning to the gaslighter. Their perception of you has been formed by what was said about you. So, they perceive your partner as your victim. They can even go as far as to tell you the stories they've shared about you are actually what others say about you.

CREATING DISTRACTIONS

When you finally get the chance to sit them down and present them with facts about their behavior, asking them to give you feedback, they'll likely distract you by changing the topic. They may even present you with another topic of discussion that implicates you, as they deem that to be of far greater importance than the feeble matters you are accusing them of. They'll do a wide range of things to avoid answering your questions. Sometimes, they'll even answer you by asking if you are convinced that your questions deserve an answer, forcing you to doubt whether the matter you wanted to address is as severe as you perceive it to be.

DIMINISHING YOUR EMOTIONS

Gaslighters will go out of their way to diminish your thoughts and feelings. They'll be the first to tell you to calm down or to get a grip on yourself when you are emotional or lashing out over their reluctance to answer your questions or address the matter. This reminds us of Mark telling Lilly to list the things she is upset about in bullet points, and he'll address them when he has time.

BLAME SHIFTING

They'll never take the blame for any friction between the two of you, and when they do, they are doing it so overtly that it is evident they don't mean it and are merely patronizing you by doing so. Having a fair and constructive discussion with a gaslighter to resolve any concerns is nearly impossible.

DENYING GUILT

Whenever you pinpoint their undesired behavior, they'll deny it entirely. They may even shift the guilt onto you for accusing them of something so terrible and question you about what kind of person you are to even think that of them. As there is no recognition of guilt, it is extremely hard for the victim—in this case—to move on from the hurt inflicted by the gaslighter's behavior.

HURTING YOU WITH COMPASSION

They'll confirm their love and affection for you, but it is not authentic and is merely a way to make you doubt yourself even more. A typical example of such behavior would be when your partner frequently flirts with other girls. When you address the matter, they'll laugh it off, saying you are jealous and crazy to think that way, as you should know how much they love you and that they are deeply devoted to only you.

IMPROVING STORIES TO COMPLIMENT THEM

They tend to make themselves the victim or the hero in the stories they share with you and the ones they share to others about you. For example, say you and your partner had a terrible argument, and they threw a vase at you. While it missed you, the shock of this behavior caused you both to stop and calm down. The next day, you may hear a different version of the story, stating that you got so upset that you chucked the vase off the counter, and they had to calm you down before you cut yourself with the broken glass:

- Do you identify with these techniques?

- Are there any other techniques you have experienced not listed here?

Week 1: Gaslighting techniques

Analyze the techniques mentioned earlier: which ones are the most familiar to you? Why are they familiar?

THE MOST LIKELY VICTIMS OF GASLIGHTING

Regardless of the kind of relationship you are in with a narcissist, you are at risk of being gaslighted. However, according to Tampa-based psychotherapist Stephanie Sarkis, gaslighting is particularly prevalent in romantic relationships—especially during the courting phase—in politics, and at the office. She also identifies certain shared features among those who are often at the receiving end of such behavior. She states that those who suffer from depression and anxiety and whose behavior portrays symptoms of attention deficit hyperactivity disorder (ADHD) are far more likely to become gaslighter victims (Dohms, 2018).

SEVEN COMMON PHRASES USED BY GASLIGHTERS

There are many phrases gaslighters use to create confusion and doubt in the minds of their victims, and the terms you may be hearing can be completely unique. That said, just as this behavior has several common traits in most cases, there are also several common phrases that are used most often and heard in such scenarios. If you are familiar with any of these phrases, it should indicate what you are up against.

YOU ARE BEING PARANOID!

This is likely the most used phrase by gaslighters across the globe. The primary intention of this phrase is to project any behavior or lies they are guilty of when you confront them. The phrase is often followed by them accusing their victims in return. The more direct your confrontation may be, the more dramatic their façade to convince you that all you know are mere fragments of your paranoia. An example would be when you accuse your gaslighting partner of infidelity, and they respond by making this statement, following it up by asking you how you can doubt how much they love you. They may even state a desperate plea that they don't know how to convince you of their love for you if you can't see it in all they do for you.

YOU ARE OVERREACTING!

This statement immediately dismisses your emotions. Whatever the situation is about, you are confronting the gaslighter who left you feeling hurt or upset. The response you may rightfully expect from someone who has the emotional intelligence to sustain healthy relationships would be to immediately calm you down and then determine what they did to put you in this state. Not the gaslighter, though. Their first response is to dismiss your emotions; next, they may imply that you are being unreasonable in your approach, as your perception of reality is entirely wrong. Let's say your partner promised you several times to attend an event with you. It can be an important work function or even a family gathering, and they don't show. This leaves you feeling humiliated, and when you express your emotions, they brush it off as nothing.

YOU ARE MAKING THINGS UP

Another version of this statement is, "It never happened." The gaslighter won't even go into precise details defending themselves against what you accuse them of. Instead, they'll dismiss your entire approach as a lie. They may even remind you of similar events in the past when you've "also made things up." Next, they may begin to tell you how grateful you should be that they stick with you, as nobody else will tolerate such behavior. Does this sound like a phrase you've heard before?

I DON'T KNOW WHAT YOU WANT ME TO SAY

This is another all-time favorite and is often accompanied by an expression of innocence and shrugging shoulders. While the previous phrase is often the response to emotionally charged accusations and questions, this is the go-to solution when you approach them calmly and collectively. A gaslighter doesn't want to answer any questions you pose to them regarding their behavior or things they've said. Rather than getting involved in a discussion to resolve matters, they'll end the conversation as quickly as possible. This phrase is often used to bring an end to calm questioning.

WITHOUT ME, YOU ARE A NOBODY!

This statement is often not the first one used in a relationship as they would much rather gradually expand their control, and this phrase is too brazen to use straight away. However, it is a phrase indicating how far your relationship has already deteriorated, as it is a downright dismissal of the victim's power and independence. By the time a gaslighter uses a phrase like this, they've already disrupted the victim's sense of reality to such a degree that they would believe these words.

YOU NEED PROFESSIONAL HELP

This phrase implies that while the gaslighter loves and cares deeply for the victim, the victim's perception of reality is so distorted that not even the love and care of the gaslighter will be able to pull them through. The only act of love they have to show is advising the victim to get help.

There are several more phrases, but I think these examples are enough to give you an idea of what is actually being said when these phrases are used in sentences. Furthermore, I want to alert you that a type of development occurs with these phrases. Initially, the gaslighter may use less brazen phrases, and you may not even notice them. But, as time goes by and your questioning intensifies, so will the types of phrases used to make you doubt yourself.

- Can you list the phrases you hear most often?

- How does hearing these phrases make you feel?

Week 1: Phrases used by gaslighters

For each phrase described above, give a score from
1 to 10 based on how often you've heard it about
yourself! Which phrases have not been described?

QUICK RECAP

- Gaslighting is a type of psychological abuse mostly present in romantic relationships, but it can also present itself in parental relations, friendships, and at work.

- By familiarizing yourself with the most common techniques and phrases used by gaslighters, you'll be able to identify this behavior before it becomes out of control.

WEEK 2

LET'S UNDERSTAND WHAT NARCISSISM, GASLIGHTING AND EMOTIONAL ABUSE ARE

After struggling for several years to get out of her narcissistic relationship with Jake, Sarah ended up in my practice. She started her story by recalling the many events during their relationship when Jake used gaslighting. At first, she wasn't aware of what he was doing or what was happening to her. She was unfamiliar with the terms "narcissism" and "gaslighting," and there was no way she could or would have identified his behavior as a means for him to gain and later sustain his power over her:

"It was our second date when it happened the very first time. I thought he was very handsome and a gentleman, and I was smitten from our first date. So, when we went on our second date, I went to even greater effort to look my best. I was wearing a new dress with a soft and flowing neckline. While we had our main course, Jake commented about my breasts being too revealing, making a nasty comment about me using my cleavage to attract interest. I was slightly offended by it. When I asked him what he meant and said that it was not nice to say, his response was that he was making a joke and it would suit me better if I could learn to take jokes with a better attitude. Then, he continued to be as pleasant and charming as before. I later doubted myself and thought maybe I was the one perceiving it all wrong. I wasn't."

This was only the first form of gaslighting that set the foundation for many years of harsh comments breaking Sarah's identity and confidence into mere fragments of what it was.

Gaslighting is not a manipulation technique limited to only narcissistic behavior, as it is also a tool used in abusive relationships or by criminals, cult leaders, and dictators (Rice, 2022). Yet, it remains a type of behavior predominantly displayed by narcissists. Researchers reveal that they estimate that five percent of the global population are narcissists (Cleveland Clinic, n.d.). Narcissism is more than merely a type of personality and is listed as 1 of the 10 listed personality disorders.

WHAT IS NARCISSISM?

Using Diagnostic and Statistical Manual of Mental Disorders, Fifth Edition (DSM-5), as the foundation of the definition of narcissistic personality disorder (NPD), we can define the type of behavior as follows ("Narcissistic Personality Disorder," 2021):

"Narcissistic personality disorder is a personality disorder where individuals have a grandiose sense of their own self-importance but are also extremely sensitive to criticism. They have little ability to empathize with others, and they are more concerned about appearance than substance. It is characterized by arrogance, grandiosity, a need for admiration, and a tendency to exploit others. Individuals with this condition often have a sense of excessive entitlement and may demand special treatment." (para. 1)

A narcissist is someone who is openly self-absorbed and extremely vain. This person has no understanding of empathy, and they are not interested or even able to provide for the emotional needs of anyone else. They are likely highly insecure about themselves, and, therefore, they get triggered easily. Some narcissists also indicate they have a persistent feeling of emptiness inside. They are incredibly competitive and arrogant about winning. They will take advantage of anyone as long as this means that they remain at the top of their power pyramid. They need an endless flow of compliments to feel good about themselves. As they have no sense of authentic self-worth, they struggle to relate with anyone who has it. NPD is a severe condition.

HOW TO SPOT A NARCISSIST?

It can be hard to spot a narcissist when you don't know what to look for in others. Another challenge that many others, like Sarah, confirm is that when you initially fall in love with the narcissist, it never crosses your mind that the person you are allowing into your life may be a narcissist. Narcissists can be very charming, and it is easy for them to win others over. They are usually leaders in their community, and as you are already in love with this person, it is easy to dismiss the warning signs. Even if you see these signs, it is only human to think that you are misreading the situation rather than considering that this person you are in love with is a narcissist.

When we discuss the following signs of a narcissist, it often happens that those recovering from a relationship with someone with NPD realize even more aspects of the person's behavior that they didn't even identify as narcissistic characteristics. If they have noticed these signs, it remains challenging to admit that they saw it but never truly comprehended whom they were dealing with.

Sometimes, they feel ashamed or embarrassed for allowing this to happen. If this is how you may feel, know that this was not your fault and that you are not alone.

AN ELABORATE SENSE OF SELF-IMPORTANCE

The narcissist's sense of self-importance exceeds vanity or even arrogance. They live with an unreal superiority, convinced that they are special and that nobody can understand their value unless they are special too. They don't approve of anything they consider mediocre and would always opt for the most expensive or luxurious options available.

LIVING IN A FANTASY WORLD

They sustain their sense of grandiosity by living in an unrealistic and imaginative world where they are convinced of their exceptional features and abilities. Narcissists consider themselves more attractive, charming, intelligent, and brilliant than anyone else. Yet, while they portray these images on the outside, inside, they are empty and alone.

DEMANDS PRAISE

To sustain such a sense of grandiosity externally while being empty inside, they need a lot of praise and compliments. They thrive as long as they are glorified, and, if the praise of others isn't enough for them, they'll only increase their self-glorification to compensate for the lack of recognition they are experiencing.

AN OVERT SENSE OF ENTITLEMENT

As they are more special than anyone else, they are entitled and expect everyone to give them special treatment. They anticipate that others will grant their every wish, and failure to do so will cause an emotional outburst. People who have shared their lives with a narcissist will also confirm that they will quickly consider you useless if you don't react quickly enough to meet their demands.

EXPLOITING YOU WITHOUT FEELING SHAME

They are superior in their eyes and therefore feel it is rightful that they expect exceptional service and solutions from others. It is why they will feel no guilt or shame to use others to get what they want without ever feeling the need to give something in return. The narcissist is convinced that taking care of their needs should be an honor for everyone else. In cases where their behavior is hurtful, they'll remain unable to show remorse due to their lack of empathy.

THEY ARE CRITICAL, DEMEANING, AND BULLIES

Whenever a narcissist feels threatened, they'll lash out and be hurtful with their comments. As they lack empathy, it is easy for them to bully even those close to them when they don't get what they want.

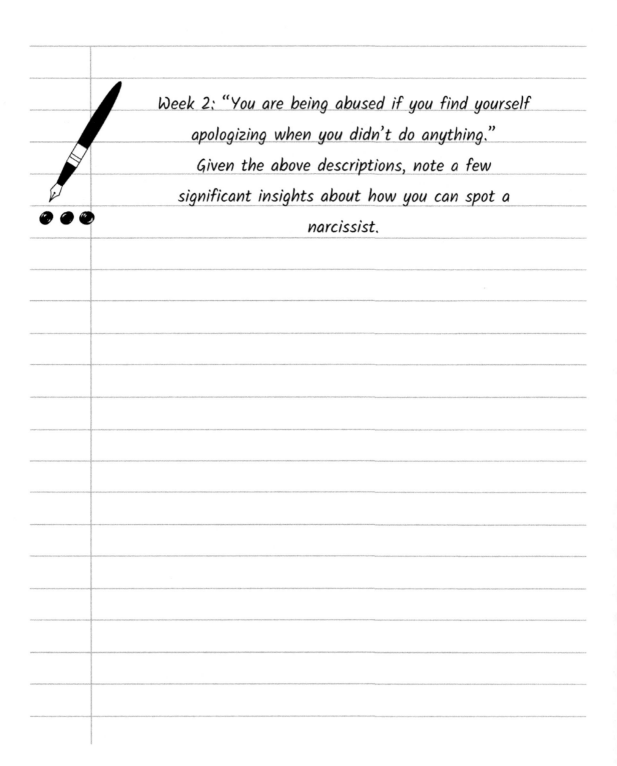

Week 2: "You are being abused if you find yourself apologizing when you didn't do anything."

Given the above descriptions, note a few significant insights about how you can spot a narcissist.

CAUSES: WHO ARE THESE NARCISSISTS?

Professionals remain unsure of the exact causes of NPD to develop, but the disorder is closely linked to various possible contributing factors.

Narcissists have often experienced some **childhood trauma**. This trauma is usually in the form of abuse and can be verbal, sexual, or physical abuse. Not all people who have suffered childhood trauma turn into narcissists, but it does appear that when it comes to NPD, it is often the case that they were hurt, and now they hurt others.

Exposure to **unhealthy relationships with relatives**. They might have felt rejected, excluded, inferior, or not worthy of love. These relationships can be with parents, siblings, or extended family.

There is also a link with **genetics**, and it appears that NPD can be hereditary.

Individual temperament and personality also play a role in the development of NDP.

As children, narcissists were most likely **hypersensitive to light**, **sound**, **and textures** during childhood also seems related.

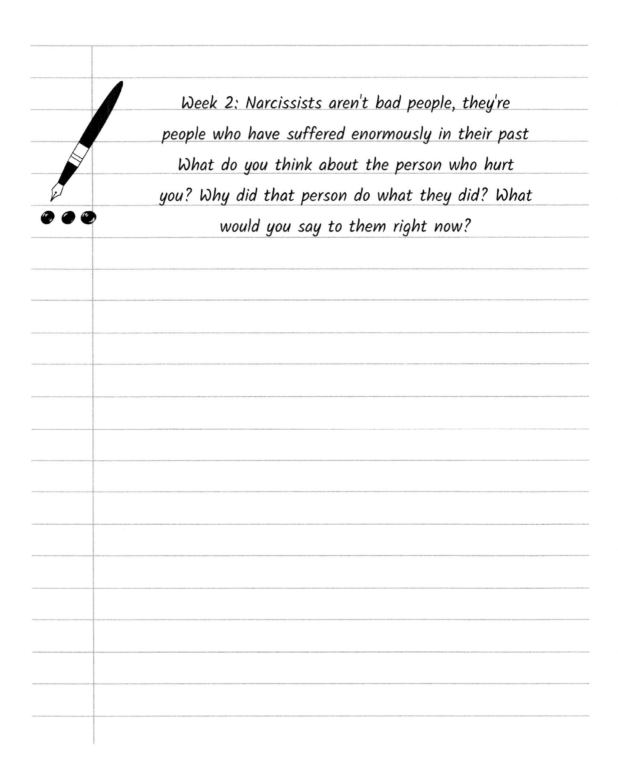

Week 2: Narcissists aren't bad people, they're people who have suffered enormously in their past

What do you think about the person who hurt you? Why did that person do what they did? What would you say to them right now?

DIFFERENT TYPES OF NARCISSISTS

Psychologists divide those with narcissism into two main categories. *Adaptive narcissists*, who portray more positive traits and can take care of themselves. They are widely considered to be helpful narcissists. It is possible for them to live a healthy life and can even contribute to the lives of others.

The other is the *maladaptive narcissist*, who is ruled by inherent toxic traits and is incapable of showing love and affection to anyone else. This category is mostly referred to when narcissism is placed under the microscope. This group can be divided into the following categories (Telloian, 2021):

- *Overt narcissists* are outgoing, competitive, entitled, in constant need of praise, and have a complete lack of empathy. This is the type of personality most people associate with NPD.

- *Convert narcissists* are vulnerable and show a low level of self-esteem. They are introverted and defensive and often avoid others as they are very insecure.

- *Antagonistic narcissists* are predominantly focused on being competitive and are very arrogant. They are often disagreeing with others and would take advantage of other people.

- *Communal narcissists* are the complete opposite of antagonistic narcissists. They are easily morally outraged and strongly react to any unfairness.

- *Malignant narcissists* are vindictive and sadistic. They quickly become aggressive and suffer from extreme paranoia.

Familiarity with the features of a narcissist and the different types of narcissism makes it easier to determine whether your concerns about someone in your life are valid:

- Can you identify which type of narcissist you have in your life?

CAN A NARCISSIST FALL IN LOVE?

It is only human to long for the person you love, or loved, to feel the same way about you. Thus, it is normal to wonder whether the narcissists you have, or had, in your life can feel love for you. Knowing that the person you've devoted yourself to did feel love for you at some point confirms that at least a part of the relationship was genuine, and all wasn't just an immense façade. Therefore, it is a valid question to ask: Can a narcissist fall in love?

The short answer would be no, they can't. Yet, we must distinguish between people with only narcissistic attributes and those who register enough on the scale to be positively diagnosed with NPD. It is essential to understand that the latter suffers from a severe mental illness. Their lives revolve around their sense of self-importance. Due to their lack of empathy towards others, it is hard for them to show authentic emotion. Yet, that said, beyond all their narcissistic layers, you'll find a person capable of falling in love like any other human being.

Being in a relationship with a narcissist is also possible while highly challenging. It is essential to understand that they will express strong feelings and that you will need to consistently encourage them to find an acceptable manner to do so.

It would be best not to argue over unnecessary matters and to learn not to react to every snide comment they may make. Furthermore, encourage them to get the treatment they need through therapy so that they can develop the necessary tools to overcome the challenges they are facing. With enough patience, perseverance, and a shared commitment to the relationship, it may be possible to have a lasting relationship with someone with narcissistic characteristics. Sadly though, acknowledging the challenges they face isn't something most narcissists would ever agree to, nor are they likely to seek help and guidance from others whose opinions they consider inferior to theirs:

- Are you in a relationship with a narcissist?

- Does your partner acknowledge the challenges they are facing?

- Are they willing to get therapy to become a better partner for you?

QUICK RECAP

- We must distinguish between those with narcissistic features and those who are registered as narcissists according to the DSM-5 definition.

- Narcissists have often been exposed to pain and are inflicting it onto others.

- Even though they come across a sense of self-entitlement, narcissists would admit a feeling of emptiness inside.

- A narcissist can fall in love, but having a lasting relationship with that person would be an immense challenge, and it demands their cooperation to improve through therapy.

WEEK 3

HEALING BY MASTERING YOUR EMOTIONS

The effects of gaslighting have a much broader impact than expected. Even the victims of gaslighting don't always realize that many of the mental, emotional, and physical challenges they are dealing with are the result of the gaslighting they are exposed to regularly.

The most common ways in which gaslighting negatively impact your life are the following:

- anxiety levels that are beyond your control

- depression

- forgetfulness

- post-traumatic stress disorder (PTSD)

- sleep deprivation

- thoughts and attempts of self-harm

- becoming socially isolated and distant from your support network

- substance abuse

- dramatic weight changes

- suicide

Week 3: Mastering by healing your emotions
It may be hard right now to figure out what you're
feeling. Choose the moods that best suit you from
the list below:

- profound sadness
- anger
- depression
- extreme anxiety
- guilt or self-blame
- shame
- hopelessness
- severe worrying
- fear

loneliness

Week 3: Ways to organize, structure, and take care

Pay attention to what you feel. If your feelings

had a voice, what would they actually say?

JENNY'S NARROW ESCAPE

If it wasn't for a nurse working in the ER where Jenny was taken to when she cut her thigh too deeply and hit a large vein, she would probably not have gotten the help she desperately needed. It was a rather unusual situation how our paths crossed. It was late afternoon when I received a phone call from a friend who is an ER doctor at our local trauma unit. He told me about this girl who came in bleeding profusely. While she claimed her injury was an accident, they could see more scars near her wound. They suspected self-harm and wanted to call in the local therapist. However, as one of the nurses was close by when the girl's partner came in, she could hear the conversation. The nurse expected to hear his shock and concern over what happened, but instead, he had an angry outburst over why she did something stupid, which meant that he had to leave his practice to come to her. She told him he didn't have to come, and then he snapped at her, saying she must think how that would harm his reputation. Her partner was a pretty well-known neurologist, and my friend was convinced that the couple would deny the help of the local therapist. Yet, he wanted me to come and see her. He was willing to hold her for a while longer before discharging her. I went, and that is how I met Jenny.

Jenny was in complete denial, or maybe it was better for her not to see the truth about her situation. She was in a relationship with someone who had the financial means to control her and had broken her self-esteem and concept of self-worth down to the point where she was sure she couldn't live without him. She confirmed that he would regularly tell her she was nothing without him. When she had panic attacks, he told her she was broken and needed professional help. Yet, he would convince her otherwise when she wanted to make an appointment, as she shouldn't waste others' time with her paranoia. It was a brutal relationship, leaving me wondering whether her visit to the ER was a suicide attempt that failed or self-harm going too far. It took the help of several friends to get Jenny into a safe house for abused women before she could start to rebuild her life and her ex-partner. He is still one of the city's most prominent neurologists. Never underestimate the immense impact gaslighting has on your life, and always remain aware that bit by bit, it eats into the foundation of your self-perception until there is nothing left to hold onto.

WHY EMOTIONAL CARE IS CRUCIAL WHEN BEING GASLIGHTED

When you are the victim of gaslighting, you must gather proof of what is being said to you or what is happening. The sole purpose of gaslighting is to remove you from reality and let you think that you are going mad. Having proof will help to keep you anchored to reality and know that you are not going insane. How you gather evidence is entirely up to you, and you'll have to do so discreetly. Even a journal can be a helpful aid to keep you connected with the truth.

If you are still in contact with family and friends, it is best to reach out to them for support. Access to a support network will also keep you from feeling isolated and alone.

When you are being gaslighted, become aware of particular routines or habits; maybe certain things always precede gaslighting. Once you can notice these signals, it becomes easier to protect yourself against this behavior.

The most crucial step you must take is to take care of your emotions. Emotional care should always be a priority in your life, and you enjoy the same degree of importance as skin or health care, for example. But, when exposed to gaslighting, it is even more essential to give emotional care the priority it deserves. Yet, as discussing our emotional health leaves us feeling vulnerable, it is often a topic we would avoid in conversation. You may experience short-term relief by ignoring your emotions, but you are causing far more severe long-term concerns.

Optimal emotional care demands that you confront any negative emotions. This may be painful, but it is the only way to establish healing and set yourself free from the hurt of being gaslighted in your life.

WHAT IS EMOTIONAL SELF-CARE?

The term refers to the time you spend identifying your deepest emotions and thoughts during quiet introspection. During such care, you'll consider how well you manage stress and how efficiently you express your feelings. The purpose of emotional self-care is to increase positivity in your life and elevate your mood. It is also proven to resolve existing concerns and dramatically improve your confidence and self-worth.

THE BENEFITS OF EMOTIONAL CARE

There are many benefits you'll be able to enjoy when you make emotional self-care a priority. These benefits will be crucial to overcoming the strain and hurt of exposure to gaslighting.

BECOMING MORE RESILIENT AND BALANCED

It will be far more challenging to remain resilient during stressful times and challenges, like when you are being gaslighted when your emotions are out of control. This happens when you have no balance and never invest time in practices helping you to reflect on your life and relax completely.

STRENGTHENS YOUR SELF-ESTEEM

During a research study at the Albert Einstein Hospital in São Paulo, scientists found that participants who have a better grip on their emotions have much stronger self-esteem and, as a result, could take on several life challenges with much greater confidence and success than participants who didn't invest time into emotional care (THC Editorial Team, 2022). Through emotional self-care, it becomes easier to identify what you want, your purpose, and how to achieve those things. This benefit can make a dramatic difference in your life, as the primary intention of gaslighting is to confuse you to create distance between yourself and reality.

IMPROVES YOUR UNDERSTANDING OF FEELINGS

As you become more aware of your feelings, it is easier to identify the emotions you experience during episodes of gaslighting and thereafter. When you are familiar with what you feel and can positively identify these emotions, the likelihood is that someone will be able to confuse you or even convince you that your perceptions are irrational.

MINIMIZES DEPRESSION SYMPTOMS

In 2017, researchers explored the impact of emotional self-care on 380 cancer patients. Their findings indicated that proper emotional self-care can drastically decrease depression symptoms even if the conditions causing these participants to be depressed didn't change (THC Editorial Team, 2022).

FIVE EFFECTIVE WAYS TO ORGANIZE, STRUCTURE, AND TAKE CARE OF EMOTIONS

As you may have minimal time to invest in emotional self-care, I share only five methods that I consider the most effective for getting a better handle on your emotions, enabling you to manage situations better when you are being gaslighted.

IDENTIFY WHAT YOU ARE FEELING

Sometimes, it happens that someone says or does something that upsets us. While we recognize the fact that we are upset, we don't identify the exact emotions we are experiencing. This lack of recognition of our actual feelings prevents us from addressing these emotions most effectively. While there is an extensive kaleidoscope of emotions we can feel, it often happens that we only focus on a few widely acknowledged ones.

Let's do a quick practice run. What are you feeling right now? Instead of saying sadness or anger, maybe you are feeling good and want to say happy. Dig a little deeper. Perhaps what you are feeling is, in fact, disappointment, confusion, rejection, isolation, excitement, or anticipation, or maybe you are furious and not just angry. Once we identify our feelings more clearly, we become more familiar with what we feel and can manage these emotions more effectively.

ACCEPT WHAT YOU ARE FEELING

The most natural response to negative emotions can be ignoring them or pretending they don't exist. Doing so usually has the opposite outcome. The more you deny the presence of a specific emotion, the more prevalent it will become. Instead, acknowledge what you are feeling and accept that it is how you are feeling now. Claim your emotion, for it is yours for a reason. Only then can you begin to explore why you are feeling this and how to resolve it.

CONSIDER THE IMPACT OF YOUR EMOTIONS

Some emotions are merely lingering on the surface, while others have a much more profound impact on our lives. This is because emotions are vibrations affecting the whole body. The stronger the emotions, the stronger their vibrations will be and the more severe their impact. Once you've identified your feelings, take stock of how it affects your life.

For example, when you've identified that you are not just sad but that you actually feel rejected, you can determine how feeling rejected influences your life. Maybe you feel less confident about doing your presentation at work tomorrow. Before you felt rejected, you could've looked forward to the challenge, but your stress and anxiety increased as you are no longer so confident in your abilities to do this well. This is how our emotions affect us negatively, touching every aspect of our lives.

KEEP A JOURNAL

Journals are wonderful tools to express your authentic emotions without judgment. It allows you to unburden yourself, but it also serves as a record where you can keep track of improvements in your life. Some prefer to never read their journals, while others use a journal to measure the progress they've made in their lives. The choice is always yours, but investing in a journal will serve you well:

- Do you have a journal?

- How often do you write in it?

- When you capture your thoughts in your journal, are you honest about your emotions? If not, why not?

If you use your journal to express yourself authentically, notice how your mood lifts when you free yourself from negative emotions while processing them through writing.

KNOW WHEN TO EXPRESS YOURSELF

You don't have to react to every emotion you experience. When you are familiar with your feelings, can identify them effectively, and have clarity on how they impact your life, it becomes much easier to determine when you'll react and when it is best to let them go. If you feel that what]your partner said while they gaslighted you was unfair—which it most likely was—you have several choices. You can get upset and feel hurt; react in anger, while this may not resolve anything; or explore the emotions you are feeling and consider every experience as an opportunity to learn more about yourself and to grow as a person. Remember—the choice is always yours.

Week 3: Ways to organize, structure, and take care
What do you think are the healthiest ways to deal
with your emotions? What would you choose to
start implementing right now?

QUICK RECAP

- A wide array of emotions can surface when you are being gaslighted.

- Negative emotions immensely impact your entire being and affect your mental, emotional, and physical health.

- If you neglect emotional care, it becomes impossible to manage your emotions, leading to them controlling you.

- Emotional care is as critical as any other type of self-care you regularly commit to.

- Through proper emotional care, you'll become familiar with your emotions, understand what you are feeling, why you are feeling it, how these feelings will affect your life, and be able to determine how to address them effectively.

- Always remember that your emotions are yours. Acknowledge them regardless of whether they are good or bad.

Week 3: The benefits of emotional care

Suppose you start being careful about how you feel. What do you think will happen next in your life?

WEEK 4

HOW TO DISCOVER YOUR TRUE REALITY

Several times over the past five years, Debra found sufficient proof that her husband, Jackson, is having sexual relationships with other women. She confronted him the first time she discovered lipstick on his shirt, and he had a perfectly good excuse for what happened. However, he had more than an excuse. He also had an accusation, questioning Debra about how little she respects their marriage even to think such a thing of him. The second time, she found an earring in her bedroom that didn't belong to her. This time, she had an emotional outburst, and Jackson told her to calm down and stop imagining things. He can remember that he bought her those earrings when he returned from a trip overseas. Now, he accused her of not caring about the things he gave her, as she forgot that it was a gift from him and lost the one.

The third time, she noticed him disappearing with a friend while they had a cocktail party at home. She hesitantly asked him where he went, and he told her to get professional help to deal with her paranoia.

Since then, Debra avoids thinking about whether Jackson is cheating on her. She removed the idea from her reality and is convinced that she only imagines things. As Jackson convinced Debra that he was not cheating on her, he was now no longer hiding the fact that he was seeing several other women.

Week 4: Reality

Think of all the lies and distortions you've heard.

Write them down below:

GASLIGHTING AND REALITY

Gaslighting reframes how you think about reality and typically uses one or a combination of the following techniques to remove the victim from reality and to distort the image they hold onto of the world:

- The gaslighter uses denial of the situation or distorts the setting or events in question.

- By isolating the victim from their support network, they lose their anchor, offering them security and certainty. This makes it easier to remove them from what is real.

- Gaslighting can also happen by shaming someone. An example of this would be when Jackson shamed Debra whenever she confronted him.

- They attack the victim's credibility, convincing them that nobody will believe what they have to say, as it is so far removed that everyone else knows they need help. For example, in the scenario recently presented, Jackson tells Debra she needs professional help to deal with her paranoia.

- At the core of gaslighting, we'll find a process known as "flipping the script." The victim may speak up regarding a valid concern they have, often backed by evidence. In response, the gaslighter effectively flips the guilt from themselves and onto the victim by questioning their reality to the degree that they don't know themselves any longer.

What techniques do gaslighters use to "flip" the guilt and distort your reality? There are several ways to achieve this, and, in some severe cases, they can actively attempt to distort your reality by doing things with the sole purpose of confusing you to such a degree, that they can control you with greater ease. Examples of such extreme behavior include planting stuff they want you to find. In Debra and Jackson's case, it can be that Jackson himself messed up lipstick on his own shirt or that he planted the earring in their bedroom to distort Debra's reality. However, in most cases, gaslighters use words or phrases to confuse the victim and gain control over them.

TYPICAL APPROACHES GASLIGHTERS USE TO DISTORT REALITY

I want to highlight the fact that there are many more examples of how gaslighters operate than what this book lends itself to mention. As the list of approaches that gaslighters follow can be pretty exhaustive, it is impossible to note and discuss every way here. Thus, the examples I share are the most commonly used options and should be a reference for how this can occur. I will hate it if you assume that what happened or is happening to you isn't gaslighting, since your situation isn't mentioned. So, when you read these examples, please put every comment or phrase you regularly hear that leaves you with a sense of discomfort under the microscope. This will help you to determine whether they are similar to what I am sharing.

The following are all phrases gaslighters use intending to distort your reality.

"If you were paying attention..." This phrase is so well crafted, for it has a dual impact on the listener. Firstly, it is an accusation that "you" were not paying attention, and that you should have, so you are already not performing according to expectation. The second blow comes with "paying attention." By stating that, it indicates that something real and relevant happened, and you missed it. Thus, whatever you perceive as reality is only in your mind, leaving the victim—you—with increased confusion and being removed from reality.

"Don't you think you're overreacting?" The problem with this statement is that it is not an accusation, yet it feels like one. But since the gaslighter only left you with a question—coupled with an assumption of what they believe about you—you can't really fight the statement they are making. Thus, you are left with doubt over your sensitivity and whether it is too much. How do you measure sensitivity anyway? And, oversensitive to whose standards?

"You always jump to the wrong conclusions." The word "always" immediately indicates that there have been previous occasions when you came to the wrong conclusion. Even if there weren't, you are now questioning your previous conclusions and will eventually convince yourself that you've identified the times when you were wrong. Once you've reached this point, it is easy to believe that you may be wrong this time again, and the gaslighter achieves what they've set out to do. You are doubting your ability to judge situations and people.

"I do this because I love you." A declaration of love, again, makes it impossible to argue the facts. It is hard to tell someone how they should love you when you are already fragile. The statement also plants a seed in your mind that what they are doing is in your best interest, and, therefore, it is the right thing for them to do.

"I am not the only one saying this." It is easy to dismiss one person's opinion, but the phrase "not the one" indicates that this is the opinion of many others too. You can't argue with the opinion of many, and the gaslighter knows that you'll never ask how many people agree with them or who these people are. Neither would you confront these people even if you get names of people who think this way. So, you are doubting yourself, and as you don't know how others see you anymore, your confidence and self-esteem wilt away:

1. Write down the phrases you are familiar with.

2. Now dissect these phrases and see their commonalities with the five examples I've provided. Ask the following questions:

    a. Can I confirm whether there is any validity to these statements?

    b. Is there any proof that these statements are factual?

    c. What are the intentions of these statements?

Everyone makes these kinds of statements from time to time. You should be concerned, though, when you hear them quite regularly. Then, you should look for a pattern in this kind of behavior.

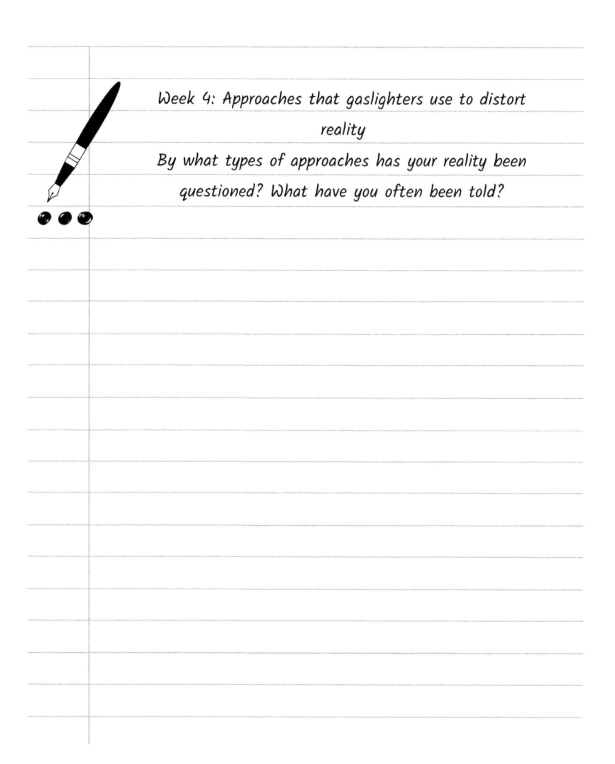

Week 4: Approaches that gaslighters use to distort reality

By what types of approaches has your reality been questioned? What have you often been told?

SEARCH FOR YOUR IDENTITY

How do you combat an attack on your perception of yourself and your reality? In this case, the best defense you can take would be an offense. Rather than justifying yourself to others or allowing others to tell you who you are, venture down a journey of exploring yourself and seeking to precisely define who you are.

The greater your clarity becomes regarding who you are and your identity, the more connected you'll feel with yourself. Thus, the chances are that the gaslighter's attempts to distort your reality will not be effective.

Week 4: Search for your identity

What are the attributes and traits that you are most proud of? What are the attributes and traits that you are less proud of?

IDENTIFY YOUR STRENGTHS AND WEAKNESSES

Essentially, your personality depends to a large degree on what you are doing well and can apply effectively in several areas of your life as well as what you are less capable of and should work on or around to achieve success. To determine this, you can consider past outcomes, think about how comfortable you feel doing certain things, and gather feedback from others to learn how they perceive you and your strengths and weaknesses.

DEFINE YOUR VALUES

What are the things you feel passionate about? What is important to you? Why are these things so important to you? By answering these questions, you'll uncover your values. Choose five or six that you consider the most important values in your life from the list of values you compile. These will be your core values and serve as a guideline for how you approach matters; respond to triggers and trauma; treat others; and allow others to treat you or talk to you.

Examples of core values are loyalty, integrity, money, love, family, success, and honesty:

- What are your values?

- Which values are the most important to you? Why is that?

You must set boundaries to protect your core values when you've identified them. What boundaries can you set to ensure that others don't overstep and disregard your values?

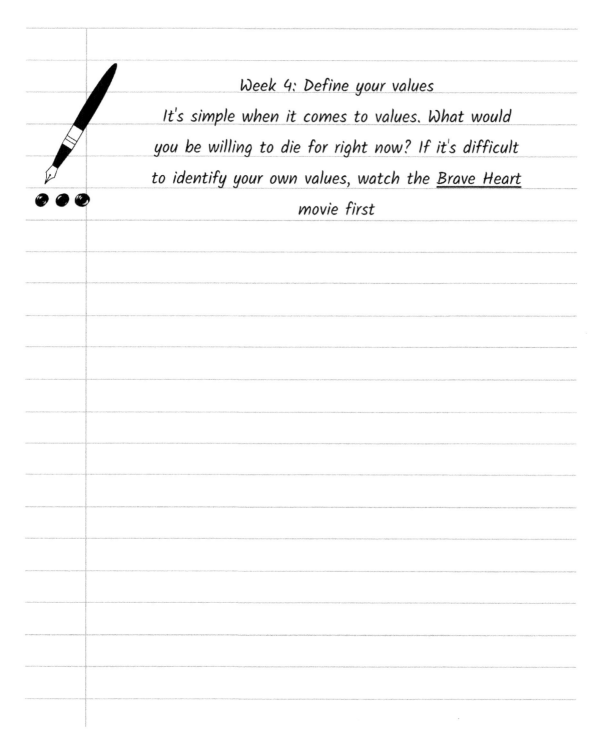

Week 4: Define your values

It's simple when it comes to values. What would you be willing to die for right now? If it's difficult to identify your own values, watch the _Brave Heart_ movie first

WHAT ARE YOUR HOBBIES OR INTERESTS?

Define the things you love doing. You feel happy and recharged afterward when you spend time doing what interests you. This gives you the energy to take on life and its challenges with more success. It will also help you to fend off the impact gaslighting will have on your emotions and the way you perceive yourself:

- What are your hobbies or interests?

- How often do you have time to do these things?

Week 4: Hobbies or interests

You don't rely on anyone. What would you like to do?

- paint
- learn how to climb
- practice a new sport
- volunteer
- learn how to ride
- run
- take evening walks
- visit new places
- read

IDENTIFY THE THINGS THE GASLIGHTER SAYS ABOUT YOU THAT BOTHERS YOU

When a gaslighter goes off and gives you their perspective on reality, it can be in stark contrast to how you perceive matters and yourself. While you'll find something slightly upsetting, there will also be statements about you that you find very unnerving and don't like to hear. Rather than addressing these matters with the gaslighter, gain additional insights from others. Ask people how they perceive you and whether they think you are a certain way. This will give you a foundation to work from and allow you to dismiss the statements made by the gaslighter or enable you to work on these aspects of your personality and grow personally.

Asking for feedback from trusted sources will also help you identify your personality in even greater detail, enabling you to connect more with who you are.

There are many other ways to define your identity and get more connected with who you are. You can even take a personality test as this would be an objective source that puts your identity into words.

HOW TO ADDRESS STATEMENTS MADE BY THE GASLIGHTER

When a gaslighter confronts you with specific statements about you that you can't question at that moment or even defend yourself again, the best approach is to remove yourself from the situation. But take note of these statements and the exact words used. Then, you can take these statements to relevant parties and determine their version of matters. You can also present to them what the gaslighter has stated and decide whether or not they agree with these statements.

Always seek the truth before you assimilate any statement about yourself or your reality. Test its validity, and if you determine the statement relevant and accurate, you can improve yourself. Discard these statements, but never allow yourself to let go of your truth, your perception of events, or how you sum up people, unless you have actual proof that you are wrong or not exactly in your observations.

NEVER CHANGE WHO YOU ARE

It would be fair to assume that when a gaslighter pinpoints certain "flaws" in your personality, it is because they would like you to improve in these areas. This is even more so when they say they tell you these things because they love you. Yet, the goal of the gaslighter is not to improve who you are for your benefit but to control you for theirs. They like to be puppet masters. As long as they get you to make fundamental changes to who you are; your social circles; how you spend your time and money; or any other aspect of your existence; they feel in control and are empowered.

Changing is not the solution for you, so hold onto your identity and who you are. Stay firm in your identity as though, if you were to change, the gaslighter's expectations will also change.

As long as Alexis and Danny have been together, Danny would tell her that she is too sensitive and emotional. He would advise her to grow a thicker skin if she wants to make it in this world. He regularly made fun of her sensitive nature when they were with others. As time passed, Alexis became so self-conscious about being too sensitive that she became emotionally numb, to the point where she stopped showing compassion and empathy when Danny was around. When he was, she would remove herself from situations where she would've wanted to show kindness rather than having Danny tell her again how overly emotional she was. In short, Alexis changed to accommodate Danny's perception of her.

Danny began to notice that Alexis was far more reserved in showing emotion, but he didn't compliment her or acknowledge that she had made changes. No, he did quite the opposite as he now accused her of being heartless and cold, stating that he can't talk to her because she feels nothing for anyone else. Sure, Alexis was taken aback and deeply hurt by these statements, yet Danny simply portrayed typical behavior for a gaslighter. Never change who you are based on the opinions and perceptions of a gaslighter.

Instead, exert yourself to get to know who you are and strengthen the connection with your identity.

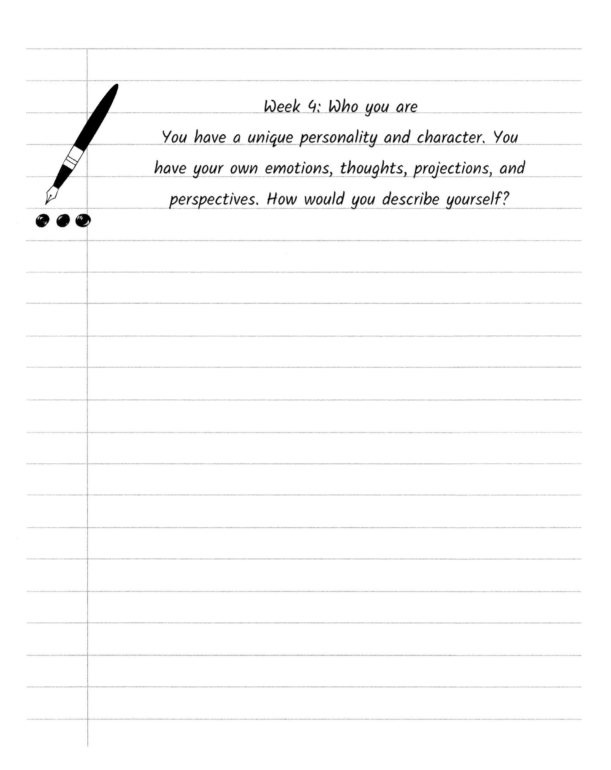

Week 4: Who you are

You have a unique personality and character. You have your own emotions, thoughts, projections, and perspectives. How would you describe yourself?

QUICK RECAP

- The greater clarity you have about who you are and the stronger your connection is with your personality, the less likely the chance that the gaslighter will be able to change your character.

- There are several common statements gaslighters use to remove their victims from reality. Identify these statements in your life and dissect them to determine their validity.

- Seek the truth about yourself and hold onto what you know is real.

- Never change who you are to please a gaslighter—they'll only change their minds again.

WEEK 5

MASTERING YOUR THOUGHTS MEANS MASTERING YOUR WORLD

When I ask people how they feel about learning certain practices and adopting new habits to master their thoughts, I get a mere blank stare. Even though the world has seen significant improvement over recent years as meditation and mindfulness have become far more known and practiced, a large part of society is still in the dark regarding meditation. They still only associate the act of mastering your thoughts as only possible when you spend hours in isolation and meditation. Some even think that it is only reserved for a select few, like monks and yogis, for example.

This is just not the case. Everyone can become the master of their thoughts and benefit from doing so. It is a process that often starts with such a simple step as thinking more about your thoughts than what you are used to doing.

THE BENEFITS OF MASTERING YOUR THOUGHTS

Would you like to enjoy greater internal peace, be able to hold your concentration for longer, be a kinder person, or be more resilient? You can enjoy these benefits when you become the master of your mind. The following are my three most valued benefits, benefits which I think everyone should have access to simply by applying themselves and learning how to control their focus.

ENJOY GREATER RESILIENCE

Being more resilient is not the same as becoming heartless and insensitive toward the needs and hurt of others. Being more resilient implies that you can remain soft and caring and show empathy without experiencing internal emotional turmoil or being drawn into an emotional whirlpool. The world is unfair, and we all need specific strategies to survive and thrive. This is what resilience does—it makes you strong enough to withstand the impact and challenges life throws at you without becoming cold, heartless, and insensitive. When you take control of your thoughts, you feel more empowered and in control of your life. You also have greater resilience, and it is with greater ease that you can overcome the challenges life presents to you.

ENJOY GREATER INTERNAL PEACE

Only when we enjoy inner peace can we process emotions and events to learn from what has happened rather than being emotionally consumed or crippled by events. Inner peace enables us to remain happy, content, and optimistic even when we confront our fears and overcome the many challenges that are just part of life.

66

RELIEVE ANXIETY

A rise in anxiety is caused by anxious feelings that spin out of control. We only have to deal with these feelings when our minds linger on anxiety-provoking thoughts; these are thoughts that always assume the worst to happen. As long as you are not in control of your thoughts and don't even notice the types of thoughts with which your mind is mainly consumed, you allow negative thoughts to determine your emotional state and evolve into even worse fear-inducing ideas. By taking control of your thoughts, you'll notice much faster when negative views enter your mind, and you can act on them. It is when you need to acknowledge their existence that you are able to replace them with positive thoughts. It is how you can minimize the prevalence of negative emotions and reduce the levels of anxiety you are experiencing. Remember that the emotions we feel, such as stomach cramps and butterflies, linked to certain feelings, may manifest physically, but these physical feelings of emotions are the result of chemicals released in the brain triggered by our thoughts:

- List the benefits you are seeking from gaining control over your thoughts.

WHEN WE ALLOW OUR THOUGHTS TO RUN RAMPANT

Every action, emotion, sensation, and condition we experience originates in our mind, or, simply put, they once were thoughts before they then become our reality. Several years ago, the author of the best-selling *The Monk Who Sold His Ferrari*, Robin Sharma, stated that everything in life is created twice. The idea first comes to mind, and only then it becomes a reality. This is a wonderfully effective way of explaining how our thoughts impact our lives and how we experience the world around us. It also alerts us of how important it is to take control of our thoughts and manage them so that they don't leave us in a state of desperation.

What happens to you when you leave your thoughts out of control? In most cases, a mind not attended to veers off in a negative direction, turning our lives upside down. While this happens, you may experience more intense stress and feel overwhelmed, anxious, and depressed. In such a state, the likelihood of substance abuse increases, your health can deteriorate, and you'll struggle or even fail to achieve your goals.

The most effective way to prevent this from happening and to feel in control of your life, but also to be actively directing it in the way you want it to go to achieve your goals, is by employing more effective management of your thoughts.

HOW TO MANAGE YOUR THOUGHTS

You can use several steps and techniques to gain greater control over your mind and manage the thoughts determining your reality. However, when we investigate this in greater detail, two key steps are at the center of effective mind control. You must employ greater awareness to identify the thoughts that you are having. The second is determining how these thoughts impact your mind and what emotions they trigger.

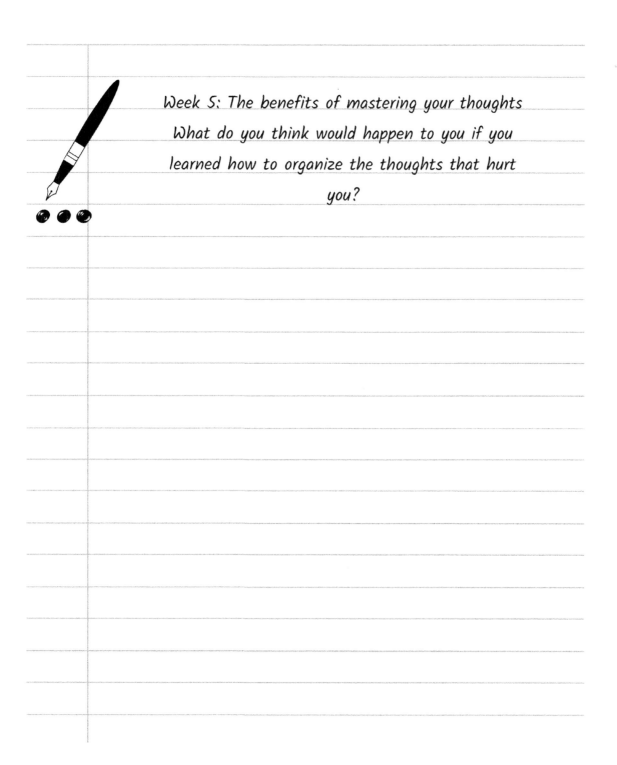

Week 5: The benefits of mastering your thoughts

What do you think would happen to you if you learned how to organize the thoughts that hurt you?

IDENTIFY YOUR THOUGHTS

Our minds have two subsections: the conscious mind and the subconscious mind. The conscious mind takes care of all our active thinking; makes decisions based on facts and evidence; and controls quite an extensive part of our lives. As the mind is bombarded with millions of stimuli eager to grab your attention, it has a technique to reduce the workload pressing on the conscious mind. It passes some repetitive choices onto the subconscious. For example, you don't have to think about whether you will brush your teeth or have coffee in the morning; your subconscious mind is familiar with your routine, and thus it simply decides on your behalf. It is an effective way to lessen the burden on your conscious mind.

The activity of the subconscious mind becomes troublesome when it identifies negative responses as your habitual reactions, and when it is triggered, it immediately responds by instilling negative emotions. Therefore, you don't even have time to consider how you would like to react at a specific time, as the subconscious decides on your behalf.

If you don't take note of these feelings that are present underneath the surface of current thoughts, you can remain in a state of unhappiness; have low confidence or self-esteem; and not even be aware of why you feel this way.

You can become aware of what is happening in your mind by being more mindful of your thoughts and what is happening in your mental space. Techniques that will help you become more mindful are yoga, meditation, or even taking a stroll in nature to clear your mind.

Week 5: How to manage your thoughts

The thoughts that hurt me the most are...

WHAT FEELINGS DO YOUR THOUGHTS CREATE

Once you get better at identifying your thoughts, you'll be able to determine how they make you feel and why they make you feel this way. This provides you with a foundation to work from as you've identified those thoughts and the impact they have, which you don't want to control you. This will make it easier to determine the thoughts you would like to have more of, which will positively impact your life. When you achieve this, you are managing your thoughts effectively.

Week 5: What feeling do your thoughts create

When I think about... I feel...

FIVE EFFECTIVE STRATEGIES TO CONTROL YOUR MIND

Taking control of your thoughts may be challenging at the start. You have no idea how to do it, and when you do, you may not be sure that you are doing it correctly. The following five strategies will serve as an excellent foundation for you to start this process, expand on it in the future, and become better at mastering your thoughts and, as a result, your life.

FAMILIARIZE YOURSELF WITH THE MIND-BODY CONNECTION

Only when you understand how the mind and the body work together—impacting each other—can you start to use the one to positively influence the other. An example of how this works would be the following situation.

Beth is under immense stress at work, and her thoughts center around her concerns that she won't be able to complete all the work she has to do before her deadline. These thoughts release chemicals that make her heart beat faster, cause her breathing to become shallower, and prompt her digestion to deteriorate as her body has a high adrenaline level, putting her in fight-or-flight mode. The fact that her thoughts increased her heart rate is evidence of the connection between her body and mind. As Beth is familiar with this connection, she also uses it to calm herself down. She deliberately takes deep, slow breaths, which is the opposite of what is happening in her mind. These breaths indicate that she is more relaxed, signaling to her mind that it should adjust its signaling to other parts of the body to relax too. Eventually, her heart rate slows and her blood pressure levels return to normal. There is a constant interplay between what is happening in our minds and what is happening in our bodies. This is happening because of the mind-body connection. Become familiar with this connection and see how you can control your thoughts through physical action.

DETERMINE YOUR THOUGHTS

When you've identified the thoughts you are focusing on, decide what you would much rather want to focus on and then manage your mind to focus on these thoughts. Practicing positive thinking instills the habit of positive thinking, favorably impacting your life.

TRY PRIMING

Do you sometimes feel like you are in a terrible mood, even though you don't really know why, and you just feel angry or sad without reason? Sometimes, it even happens when you wake up in the morning, and while you know you have no reason to feel this way, you still do. These moments call for priming.

Priming is simply a technique to bring your thoughts to the moment. By doing so, you can manage what is taking place in your mind.

You can give priming a go right away:

1. Sit in a comfortable position and note how you are feeling physically.

2. How is your body feeling? Do you experience pain or discomfort? Maybe you are hungry.

3. Don't judge how you are feeling; just become aware and acknowledge everything you are feeling. By doing this, you are bringing your thoughts to the present, and when we do, we relax physically and mentally as the present is a stress-free space. By practicing priming regularly, you practice managing your thoughts, and gradually it will become an intuitive action.

USE VISUALIZATION

Waking up from a beautiful dream is refreshing and leaves us feeling optimistic and great about the day. Visualization is a lot like dreaming, but a predominant difference is that we determine what we'll be dreaming about when we visualize. Thus, visualization is a way to define our dreams and—as things happen, first in the mind and then in reality—to realize what we desire. By practicing visualization, we become comfortable with managing our thoughts and can determine what we want from the future.

Week 5: Effective strategies to control your mind

Of those described the preferred strategy is...

It suits me best because...

I could apply it when...

QUICK RECAP

- The type of thoughts you have will determine the kind of life you'll have. Therefore, you need to manage your thoughts effectively.

- When you have control over thoughts, you can determine the kind of life you want, the state of your relationships, and how happy you will be overall.

- As long as we permit our thoughts to control us, we will remain in an emotional, mental, and physical state of despair.

- Meditation, visualization, and priming are only some of the strategies you can follow to better manage your thoughts.

- The more you practice managing your mind, the more naturally it will come to you.

WEEK 6

HEAL BY STARTING TO MAKE DECISIONS AGAIN

66 The last major decision I made for myself was the day I decided I had enough and the relationship was over. It felt like such an immense breakthrough. I felt free, and I was hopeful. I thought I would give myself a year to get my life back on track. Well, it is now one year and eight months later, and I still haven't made any other major decisions. It feels like I am mostly procrastinating on every choice that I come across. My inability to decide is the most relevant concern I have now. I struggle to move on, and I don't know why. Honestly, this is not what I expected to happen."

This frustration was shared by one of my patients during her first appointment. She's not alone. Once you've managed to break free from a relationship with a gaslighter, it is normal to feel the desire to transform your entire life. Yet, transformation demands some serious decisions, and as you struggle to make any finite choices, transformed may hardly be the correct word to describe your life. What makes this situation even more desperate is that you start to wonder whether your gaslighter was right when you were told that you'd be nothing without them. If you identify with this situation, let's immediately stop this self-inflicted pain.

You are not the only person feeling disheartened by your inability to decide. What you are experiencing is a normal consequence of long-term exposure to gaslighting, making dealing with it a part of your healing journey.

WHY IS IT SO HARD TO DECIDE?

Gaslighting isolates you from your support network, leaving the victim vulnerable and alone. It also eats into your confidence; lowers your self-esteem and self-worth; and leaves you disempowered. These are all contributing factors to the high prevalence of depression and anxiety in gaslight victims, which is also why you struggle to make decisions. You lack confidence, and as you are treading on the journey ahead with uncertainty, it is much harder to make progress. It can also be that you haven't reconnected with your previous support network or even feel that you can't connect with them as there were things said and feelings were hurt. As your trust in others is shattered, forming similar bonds with new people may be challenging. It is hard to establish bonds when trust is lacking. Therefore, it may be that you have nobody who you trust to bounce your decisions off, and this makes making choices even harder:

- Have you been isolated from your support network?

- Are you struggling to form new bonds with others?

- Are you feeling too vulnerable to make any choices but frustrated with your inability to decide and make progress you desire?

Week 6: Why is it so hard to decide?

It's hard for me to decide because...

FEAR AND DECISION-MAKING

Another contributing factor deserving of attention is the fact that fear is a very relevant emotion to experience while being trapped in a gaslighting situation, and it has a lasting power that will only dissipate as time goes by and when you address your fears directly. Fear can have a debilitating impact on your ability to make decisions.

There is a biological explanation to it all. When you are in a state of fear, your body enters survival mode. Your ability to protect yourself from imminent danger improves as your eyesight sharpens and circulation to your muscles increases, enabling you to be faster and stronger; but other brain functions, not directly linked to survival, slow down. The entire biological process is regulated by your hormones. The amygdala is the brain's most relevant part when you are in survival mode. While an active amygdala can save your life, it will slow down the capacity of other brain parts vital for decision-making (Delagran, n.d.). It just means that even if you want to make decisions, you may not be physically capable of doing so until you've addressed the fear you are experiencing.

JASON'S STORY

Jason grew up as the only child of his single mother. His dad committed suicide when he was only four years old, and he can hardly remember anything about his father. What he does remember was his mother always blaming his dad for everything that went wrong in their home. It could be anything from a drain being clogged, to her losing her job at the local ice cream parlor. His mother convinced him that his dad was a terrible man. That was his reality until his dad's family finally made contact with him again when he was ten. Then he heard another side of the story.

When he questioned his mother about his father and everything she said about him, he flipped a switch in her mind. She now turned her gaslighting toward her son. It started with her turning his questions about her statement, referring to his dad, onto him. She would tell him that she never said terrible things about his dad and that it was not her fault he understood her wrong and opted to believe all that was bad about his father. She even told the young Jason that a child who can think so poorly of his deceased father must have something seriously wrong with his mind. She would also continue to say that his dad's family is putting utter nonsense in his head and that she doesn't even know what he is talking about.

On several occasions, she even booked sessions with a therapist with Jason. But as she instilled so much fear in him related to what he should expect from such a visit, he begged her to cancel the appointments and promised to stop asking her about his father.

His mother's behavior left Jason feeling scared, confused, and helpless. He was a mere child who was no longer sure what his mother said about his father and what was real or who was lying to him. As he had nowhere to go, he had to take his mother's version as the truth. Her gaslighting of Jason only worsened as he aged until he was finally old enough to leave home. When Jason got the freedom he hoped for, he struggled immensely to make any decisions. He couldn't decide where he wanted to stay, what career he wanted to have, or if he wanted to study. Jason worked for 4 years flipping burgers and earning minimum wage, simply because he couldn't decide what he wanted to do with his life. When he finally made up his mind, it was due to his girlfriend's support that he could choose where to apply to study after another 18 months.

Jason's inability to decide placed immense stress on him, his relationships, and his girlfriend's life. It was also her who got him so far to get help later on, and he would work through his fears with therapy. Today, Jason can look back on that time, understanding what happened to him and with relief that it is over.

Week 6: Jason's story
Why was Jason afraid to decide? What do you
think about your difficulty deciding?

REFLECT AND LEARN

The answers we seek to the difficult questions that keep our thoughts at ransom or mostly trapped inside are why you need to allow time to reflect. It is when you can identify mistakes you've made in the past that you'll be able to begin finding these answers. Only when you've identified what you've done wrong can you improve and become better, gaining confidence in your ability to decide. During such reflection, you can also determine what the things you are responsible for are and which obstacles you are facing with making choices are caused by the gaslighting you've experienced. I am sharing seven steps in identifying and learning from past mistakes to recover from your inability to decide.

STEP 1—ACKNOWLEDGE YOUR MISTAKES

When you acknowledge your mistakes, you'll be able to identify what mistakes you are actually to blame for and what are the ones the gaslighter only shifted onto you as part of their typical behavior. Of course, you need to address your mistakes by making things right again. If you must apologize to someone, do the necessary. Apologizing is a powerful act, as taking responsibility for your mistakes increases the confidence others have in you and what you have in yourself:

- What mistakes that you have made that you know you need to apologize for? Do so as soon as possible, and kick off the progress you desire.

STEP 2—REFRAME YOUR MISTAKES

Step back from the situation and observe your actions from a distance. Determine why you've made a mistake; why it was the wrong thing to do or say; and how your choice was guided by the circumstances or your beliefs.

STEP 3—WHAT HAVE YOU LEARNED

Identify the lessons you've learned while observing your behavior from a distance:

- How do these lessons help you to improve your future behavior?

- What can you do better next time around?

STEP 4—TAKE ACTION

Lessons without accompanying action are meaningless. You have to proceed and take the steps you've identified to progress as planned.

List three steps you can take right away to start progressing toward a space where you are confident in your decisions.

STEP 5—MONITOR YOUR PROGRESS

Check in regularly to see if you are progressing as you've envisioned and are improving your behavior.

STEP 6—ACKNOWLEDGE THAT VULNERABILITY IS OKAY

It is human to feel vulnerable and scared at times. If you feel this way, it can be easy to consider yourself still under the influence of your gaslighter, which may put additional stress on you. Yet, it is not the case. Vulnerability is a normal human emotion; the best way to address it is to admit your feelings and embrace them as part of your journey.

STEP 7—ACCEPT THAT YOU'LL BE MAKING MORE MISTAKES

Mistakes are part of our nature. Regardless of how hard we try to avoid mistakes, we'll always make some as we are all just touching in the dark. Mostly, it is going well, but we sometimes lose focus and err in our behavior, choices, and words. Stop beating yourself up over it. Instead, focus on your improvement.

THE THREE MOST RELEVANT THINGS PREVENTING DECISIONS

While fear, vulnerability, a lack of confidence, and low self-esteem can all inhibit your decision-making ability, they aren't the only obstacles that can keep you from making vital decisions regarding your life.

LACK OF INFORMATION

If you don't have sufficient information to make an informed decision, you'll not be able to progress to the point where you can make a decision. This may not be due to your history of being gaslighted but simply because you need more information to make a good choice. Overcome this obstacle by gathering more details until you thoroughly understand your options and the context, enabling you to decide:

- Consider the most critical decision you are procrastinating on and determine whether you have enough information to make an informed choice. If not, make gathering more information your prime priority.

TOO MUCH INFORMATION

Sometimes, the opposite is also the case. Having access to too much information can be overwhelming and confusing, causing you to procrastinate in your decision-making. When you have an overwhelming amount of information, it can be easier to be misled by information, as it is harder to determine what is authentic and what is not. Overcome this challenge by calling on the support of others you trust to help you with guidance on what information is relevant and should guide your decisions:

- Who can you call for advice, guidance, or bounce your ideas off?

- Set up a meeting with this person or these people as soon as possible.

EMOTIONAL ATTACHMENT

The third factor, even though many more factors can affect your decision-making ability, is how emotionally detached you are from the situation. When you are too emotionally attached or not emotional at all, it can be that you may struggle to progress from your stagnant position. Once you link a balanced emotional response to the outcomes of your decision, you can move from the place of "deciding not to decide," which may be your current state.

TAKING SMALL STEPS

When you want to accomplish significant shifts in your situation, small but sustainable steps will get you much further than making a few immense changes you can't keep up with. Therefore, when you step out of a gaslighting relationship, it would be best to avoid making any significant decisions. Rather than continuing persistent procrastination that only increases the stress level you are already experiencing, opt for making a few minor changes.

Examples of how you can bring minor changes into your life are changing away from the brands you'll usually purchase when grocery shopping or changing your routine slightly. Maybe challenge yourself to make one decision every week that will result in a different outcome than what you are used to.

By continuously making small changes, you've become comfortable with the process and soon find yourself making much more impactful decisions with much greater ease:

- List several minor decisions you can make and practice during the next couple of weeks.

Week 6: Taking small steps

I want to decide to...

The first steps I want to implement are...

QUICK RECAP

- After you've decided to move on from the gaslighting relationship, you may not make any other decisions again.

- Struggling with decision-making is normal when you feel vulnerable, your confidence is shattered, or when you are afraid.

- A lack of information, too much information, and your emotional involvement in your decision can also impact your ability to decide.

- Determine through introspection what is holding you back from choosing, then address these concerns through changes in your behavior by making small but consistent decisions.

WEEK 7

HEALING AND GETTING BETTER BY DETACHING

Radio silence is the best approach to breaking free and staying disconnected from a gaslighter.

Dr. Stephanie Sarkis explains it as follows (Sarkis, 2018):

"There are ways to decrease a gaslighter's influence in your life. Many of these will boil down to one thing: Get as far away as possible. Because gaslighters are so slippery and manipulative, your best bet is to cut off all contact. If you can't completely cut off contact, drastically reduce it." ("So, What Can You Do?" para. 2)

When you've been in this kind of relationship for a long time, you may be convinced to believe that the toxic behavior you are exposed to is nothing but a mere cry for help and that you can't leave the person who's poisoning your mind and life. As the primary purpose of this kind of behavior is to distort your reality, you may even doubt your observations, wondering if how you perceive matters is truly how it is. These are probably the most influential factors making it hard to break free. However, there are several valid reasons why breaking away from a relationship where you are regularly exposed to gaslighting behavior is vital, as it is such a toxic place to be.

THREE REASONS WHY YOU SHOULD BREAK FREE FROM YOUR ABUSER

Gaslighting can be prevalent in any relationship, but it is far more common in romantic relationships. It is also far more common that victims of such abuse have a choice to leave their abuser when this occurs in a romantic relationship. For example, it is much more possible for an adult male or female to walk out of such a toxic relationship than for a child stuck with a gaslighting parent. This is mostly due to adults having a much greater independence than the minor trapped in a toxic parental home. Yet, sometimes victims struggle to make this break and set themselves free, even if they have the financial or physical means to do so. We must explore why this happens, especially as so many patients share their frustration that they haven't made a move to break free earlier in the relationship. I am expanding on the most common reasons they state for staying longer than they ever should've.

Week 7: Three reasons

The reasons why I need to detach myself can be expressed as follows:

THEIR APOLOGIES MEAN NOTHING

Gaslighters are masters at apologizing without actually apologizing. Yet, their victims consider it a sincere apology as they get stuck at the acknowledgment of the other that they are sorry. Here, we can look at several examples of apologies like, "I am sorry you feel that way," or, "I regret that it is how you perceived it." Neither of these is an authentic apology. A genuine apology doesn't say sorry for something "you" did. It is saying "I" am sorry about something "I" did. When they apologize for how you feel, they still blame you for being upset. If you are still stuck in such a toxic relationship, please, don't allow yourself to believe such insincere apologies any longer.

The second concern regarding apologies is that the gaslighter may say sorry but won't change their behavior. Always remember that an apology lacking action to improve behavior is mere manipulation:

- How many apologies have you heard, stating regret over what you've done, or felt?

- Next, reflect on the past behavior of your gaslighter and determine if their apologies ever bring about changes in their behavior.

THEY EMPLOY YOUR WEAKNESSES AGAINST YOU

When you enter into a relationship with a gaslighter, they may come across as the most caring person you've ever dated. They made you feel safe and protected, and it was easy for you to share your weaknesses and be vulnerable. While you were trusting your deepest emotions, the person was gathering information to use at a later stage.

I want to stop our line of discussion here for a moment. It may not have been an intentional act. Not all gaslighters are even aware of what they are doing. They merely consider their behavior as the way to behave and as being perfectly acceptable. So, I am not stating that all gaslighters are out to get you; it is just who they've become. It is not up to you to change them, especially if they can't even see what they do is wrong. We don't have as much power over one another to instill profound personal change in another. Change comes from within.

Now, once they have this information, they have power over you. They will hit you where it hurts, as it is already a vulnerable spot. Let me share snippets of Cindy's story to help me clarify this.

Cindy had just turned 30 when she divorced her husband and the father of her three-year-old son. They were married for 6 years before her ex-husband's behavior became so concerning, she feared he might do something to her or their son. Needless to say, Cindy felt vulnerable. She never saw herself as a single mother, so she sought security. She found that in the arms of James. She took her responsibility to care for her child very seriously and, instead of leaving her son with caregivers, opted to meet people in the safety of her home through online dating. This is where she met James—also recently divorced—who had a young daughter. He came across well, and after they'd chatted online for a while, they met in person. After dating for several months, James moved in, and they got married. Cindy felt that she finally found the security she desperately sought and shared every detail of her life with James. As time passed, James changed—or his true nature revealed itself. He wanted control over Cindy, and if she disagreed, he would blast her with threats to attack her vulnerabilities. He would make statements about how she won't make it on her own. He would often ask her what kind of mother she would be to her son divorcing a second husband. As her son's dad was always watching to see where she would make a mistake, James would convince Cindy that leaving him would give her first ex-husband enough ground to claim primary care over their child. Cindy stayed in that marriage for 9 years, often doing the impossible to keep the peace and ensuring her son had a safe and relatively stable environment to grow up in. It only was when he turned 16 that she told her son that she wanted to leave James, and that was when she finally managed to walk away from James's toxic behavior.

THEY SURROUND THEMSELVES WITH PEOPLE WHO ADORE THEM

Unless you are in a relationship with a gaslighter, you may never know what kind of person they truly are. Generally, they come across as the nicest people you can imagine having as friends. Thus, there are enough people who like them, and they make sure that they surround themselves with those who think the world of them. Anyone who confronts their behavior will be pushed out without them even thinking twice about it.

Essentially, it is much harder to walk away from someone when everyone in that person's life convinces you how lucky you must be to have them in your life. This makes it very hard for you to come to terms with the fact that detaching is the only way out of the abusive relationship.

WHEN YOU DON'T DETACH

Detaching may be challenging. Going into radio silence and sustaining it will also be challenging. You may even find that after years after cutting all contact with your gaslighter, they may resurface and see if you'll let them in again. Don't, for they never truly change. They may only come across as if they've changed, but the only true reason why they are knocking on your door once again is that they've been unsuccessful in getting similar results with others as they did with you. Nevertheless, staying in a relationship with such a toxic person and refraining from detaching can be much more complicated than detaching.

CRUSHING YOUR SELF-ESTEEM

The process can take place gradually, and you may not notice how you lose your independence or your confidence is shrinking. Still, the longer you stay in this relationship, the more you are constantly exposed to active efforts to crush your self-esteem, as that is how they maintain complete control over you. It is possible to rebuild your self-esteem and even to come out stronger than before, but it is a challenging and time-consuming process that you could've avoided. You'll also not likely be able to rebuild this until you've left the gaslighter in your life.

INCREASED ISOLATION

The social impact of isolation is quite evident. When you become isolated from your loved ones, your relationships will suffer. There are various ways the gaslighter accomplishes this distance, and some of these can be hurtful to yourself or your loved ones, scarring bonds so severely that they'll never heal. It is not where the risks of isolation end—it also impacts your emotional, mental, and physical health as you become more anxious, sad, depressed, and stressed. This affects the body in several ways, varying from poor quality sleep to high blood pressure and increased heart rate. Those isolated are at greater risk of feared diseases like Alzheimer's and dementia (Caporuscio, 2020).

MENTAL HEALTH CONCERNS

Records indicate an increased risk of several mental health concerns like anxiety, depression, and trauma when victims experience prolonged exposure to gaslighting (Nall, 2020).

When recalling Cindy's story, it is apparent these are all symptoms that revealed themselves to a certain degree in Cindy. As she experienced such destructive behavior, it took her quite some time to reach a point where she could love herself, reach out to her family, reconnect with them again, and feel confident in the person she is. What took her much longer to overcome was the regret she had over wasting such a large part of her life living in a relationship that was so bad for her and her son. Cindy had good intentions all along, but that wasn't a sentiment shared with her now ex-husband.

Week 7: When you don't detach

In the past, when I didn't detach myself, I suffered in the following ways...

In the future, some things could be affected...

FIVE EFFECTIVE STRATEGIES TO DETACH FROM YOUR ABUSER

It may be hard to break free from a gaslighter's toxic grip on you, but it isn't impossible. Before taking steps that will constitute an immense change in our lives, it remains vital to clarify why you are doing this before proceeding. So, before you make the changes needed to detach yourself, I want you to ponder why you want to break free and what your life would look like in five years if you don't make these changes. When doing so, being as comprehensive as possible with your list for change is unexpectedly challenging, and you may want to revert to your list during tough times.

KEEP THE BREAKUP CONVERSATION QUICK

Don't draw this conversation out, as they will eventually wear you down, and the chances are that you'll give in, making it much harder to reach this point again. So, prepare yourself, plan your exit, and ensure this is a short conversation, stating that you've had enough and that the relationship is over. Don't leave them any room to wiggle themselves out of this situation.

NEVER TRUST THEIR PROMISES

You may be bombarded with promises of how they'll change and how much they'll do to make you happy again. Don't believe it—these promises are mere forms of manipulation. You may even be confronted with reminders of what a fantastic team you are, and the gaslighter may even ask you how you threw away your relationship like it had no meaning. That, too, is merely a technique to keep you from detaching.

GO INTO COMPLETE RADIO SILENCE

Do not allow any form of communication between yourself and the gaslighter. When you are going through a divorce involving minor children, direct all communication to your attorney. I can't emphasize this enough; don't allow text messages; phone calls; emails; and definitely no visits, chats, or coffees. Also, block them from your social media platforms, as this, too, can become a means of communication.

GET YOUR SUPPORT NETWORK ON BOARD

There will be times when you doubt your decision, feel vulnerable, and think back on the times when you believed your relationship was good. During these times, it will be challenging to stick to your decision. Rather than giving in during moments of weakness, ask your friends to remind you of how bad your relationship was; they can keep you upright, standing firmly in your decision.

Week 7: Five effective strategies to detach from your abuser

I will try to stand out using the following strategies:

It might prevent me from detaching...

COMPILE A LIST OF ALL THE REASONS WHY

Why did you conclude that the only way to save yourself is detachment? Make this list as comprehensive and expressive of your emotions as possible. If your weakness overcomes you in the middle of the night and you don't want to wake up your friends, turn to your list. The reasons on that list are why you need to remain strong for yourself and those who love you and want to see you happy.

QUICK RECAP

- Staying in a relationship with a gaslighter harms your emotional, mental, and physical well-being.

- The only way out of such a toxic relationship is through detachment.

- Decide why you want to leave, establish your support system, and pull the plug on the relationship with a quick but potent conversation to set yourself free.

WEEK 8

HEALING BY FINDING YOUR OWN IDENTITY

The most conventional answer you'll get when you would have to ask people on the street what their identity is would be to tell you what they do for a living. However, that only refers to their careers or jobs and is a mere fraction of their identity. Most people have only a vague understanding of who they are and struggle immensely to capture their identity in words. When we look at relationships where gaslighting is present, it is clear that identity is the part of the victim mostly under attack. So, before we explore how abuse and manipulation—typically present in such a relationship—impact your identity, let's delve into precisely defining what your identity entails.

WHAT IS IDENTITY?

In the most simplistic definition, we can capture the term as referring to a culmination of all the relationships you have in your life. These relationships go back to your childhood, and some may no longer exist, yet they contributed to forming you into the person you are today. For example, your relationships with your parents, siblings, childhood friends, and teachers contributed to your present-day identity. But it is even more than that. It also refers to certain outside factors you can merely accept, like your culture, age, and even the religious beliefs you were brought up in, as these all impact the choices you make today.

On a more complex level, identity also refers to your values defining your choices. We can also include the roles you fulfill, of which your position in your career or job is merely one aspect. Other roles you fulfill are being a mother, father, brother, friend, son, or any other similar relationship status you may have.

It is also impossible to determine your identity at one age and expect it to remain stagnant. When we see what most of the prestigious psychologists, whose work we study today, state about identity, it is evident that it is far more complex. Erik Erikson noted that the "ego identity" remains stable throughout our entire lifespan, but that there are also changing versions of oneself depending on one's life stage. Sigmund Freud divided identity into three entities: the id, ego, and superego. In Freud's definition, the *id* refers to the essential parts of our personalities driving us forward; these are what many would refer to as our animal instincts. The *superego* is the part of identity inspired and managed by the values you sustain and your morality. Lastly, the *ego* is where the two extreme versions of the self meet in moderation and where you'll find your true identity ("Identity," n.d.).

As a large part of your identity is determined by your relationships and experiences in life, it is only natural that exposure to the abuse of a gaslighter will have a profound effect on your identity.

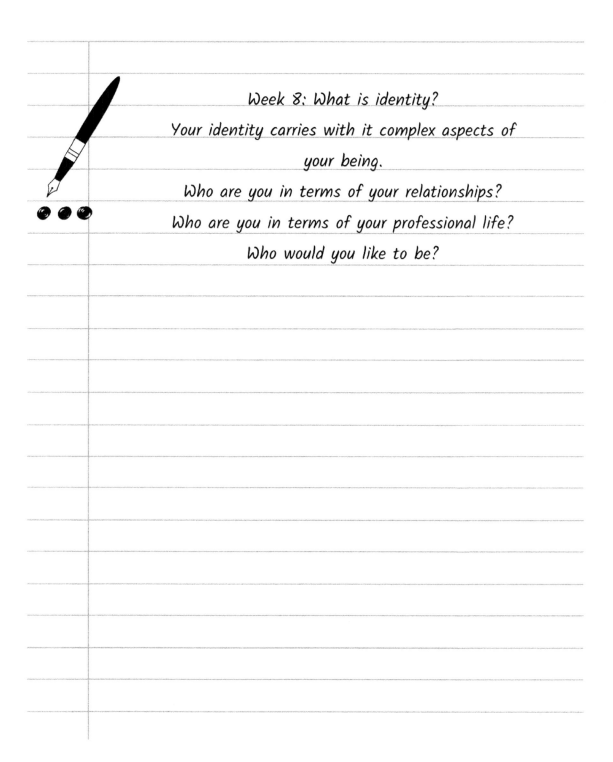

Week 8: What is identity?

Your identity carries with it complex aspects of your being.

Who are you in terms of your relationships?

Who are you in terms of your professional life?

Who would you like to be?

ABUSE AND MANIPULATION STEALING YOUR IDENTITY

Is this maybe too much of a harsh statement to make? I don't think so. When you suffer abuse or the manipulation at the core of gaslighting, you are exposed to events, conditions, experiences, and emotions determining your values. The relationships you have from early onwards in your life—especially if this is the kind of relationship you grew up in—are different and, thus, impact you in a way that affects your identity.

When we consider Erikson's expertise, stating that identity changes as we go through various stages of life, we have to remember that even the adult's identity is at risk. For example, you may have had the most amazing relationships with your relatives growing up in a loving and stable home, but long-term exposure to gaslighting in an adult relationship will affect your identity in the present and onwards.

EMMA'S STORY

Emma's story is a perfect case study to determine how manipulation and abuse can steal your identity as an adult and even more so during childhood.

Emma grew up in a loving home as the youngest in the family. She has a brother, two years older than her, who is very protective over his younger sister. When Emma left home for college, she had certainty about who she was. She has always been an avid artist and was fortunate enough to be accepted into one of her home state's most prestigious art departments. Everyone who knew Emma would define her as an upbeat, bubbly girl who is confident in her talents, with good reasons, as she was highly talented. She had big plans to open an art gallery and was already exhibiting since she was only fifteen. Emma's identity was quite well-defined.

At college, she met Kevin. Kevin was a law major and planned to become a big-shot attorney. His identity was also well-defined, or so it came across. He was as driven as Emma, and the two quickly became a happy and content couple until

Emma's first exhibition was too successful for Kevin's liking. He felt that her success made others oversee him and his gaslighting became very prevalent. Gradually, he would make remarks that made Emma doubt her ability to deliver exceptional art. As time passed, she became less confident in her ability and less upbeat. Emma was no longer sure what she wanted to do with her life and gave up on her studies. She stayed on merely to be close to Kevin, who presented himself as the one protecting Emma from making a fool of herself, thinking her art was exceptional while, in "reality," it was merely mediocre. Emma's values, beliefs, viewpoint, and entire self-perception changed.

That is how Kevin managed to steal Emma's identity with abuse and manipulation.

HOW IDENTITY IS FORMED

Forming your identity takes time, and while you may not be actively aware of it, it stretches across most of your childhood years right into adolescence and after that.

We can break identity formation into three essential tasks or concepts ("Identity," n.d.). Initially, there is when you discover your potential; this happened to Emma when she realized that she had this extraordinary talent to do art. Discovering her potential also defined her purpose in life, guiding her to seek opportunities to improve her potential and become better at what she is already good at:

- What are the first things you know you are good at? Maybe it has been a while since you last practiced any of these things, but it doesn't matter. Even if many years have passed since you immersed yourself in these things, write them down now.

Add to that how these things determined the plans you had for your future.

While defining your identity, the second task is linked to your relationships. Emma grew up in a loving home with her parents and a brother who adored her. Through these relationships, values like mutual respect, empathy, kindness, and humility became part of her identity:

- How would you define your relationships during childhood, adolescence, and adulthood?

The third leg of the process is linked to experimentation, especially during adolescents. Emma exhibited her art at an early age, and in that way, she experimented to determine the feedback she got from strangers defining how well others perceived her art:

- What experimentation during your childhood years impacted your identity?

Forming your identity is a process that requires time. Even as an adult, you won't be able to redefine yourself in the wink of an eye. Therefore, it is best to be alert to any changes to how you define yourself and to take counteraction as soon as possible.

SIGNS INDICATING MANIPULATION ARE ROBBING YOU OF YOUR IDENTITY

Some of these signs are very evident in Emma's story, but as you read through the following list, see which of these signs are present in your life:

- missing out on opportunities that would typically have excited you

- becoming stagnant in your career

- your mind is consumed with what the other person will say

- feeling a sense of discomfort in your skin

Do you experience any of these signs?

Reading these signs here is just written confirmation of something you may already be aware of but remain uncertain of how to address it effectively.

Week 8: Signs indicating manipulation and robbing...

I realize my identity was stolen because...

SEVEN STRATEGIES TO FIND YOURSELF AFTER BEING A NARCISSIST'S VICTIM

If your hand is up as someone who's aware that you've lost a large part of yourself in a gaslighting relationship, the following seven strategies will help you rebuild your identity. Nevertheless, be patient and kind to yourself. This is a lengthy process, but as long as you continue progressing, you are on the right track.

ACKNOWLEDGE WHAT HAPPENED

Denying that you are feeling the consequences of what happened to you will only prolong healing. The more we want to avoid specific topics, the more relevant they become in our lives until they entirely consume our thoughts, actions, and behavior. So, the first step to recovery will be to admit that your relationship did rob you of your identity. Acknowledging this may leave you with a sense of sadness or even the desire to mourn the person you used to be. Allow yourself space for that to happen, but remember that you are on the verge of rebuilding yourself. The longer your mourning takes, the longer it will be before you can rebuild your identity:

- Are you ready to acknowledge the damage your identity suffered from this abuse?

- If you are ready, share these feelings with someone you trust.

SURROUND YOURSELF WITH A SUPPORTIVE CROWD

It is difficult to determine, define, and rebuild your identity. There will be times when you may feel exhausted or hopeless. Therefore, surround yourself with people who care and want the best for you. The people who encourage you in your journey become genuinely invaluable to your recovery:

- Can you identify your crowd by adding names to a list of people who support you?

- If you struggle to find people you trust, joining a support group in your area may be helpful. Determine whether there are any such groups around where you can join in.

IDENTIFY ONE THING YOUR NARCISSIST SAID YOU CAN'T DO— THEN DO IT

What are the limitations that were said for you? Pick one thing you were repeatedly told you were unable to do, and make it your priority to do it. It is immensely fun and incredibly empowering to break through these barriers.

DEFINE AND COMMUNICATE YOUR BOUNDARIES

Our identity is always vulnerable to outside forces. Therefore, it is vital that you set barriers to protect what is important to you and define how you will clarify these barriers. You must keep what is yours. Boundaries determine what type of behavior you will tolerate or how much of yourself you are willing to give to a cause. For example, you expect people to address you with respect when they talk to you, and if someone doesn't, you point out to the person that it is not a way you'll allow anyone to speak to you:

- First, identify what you want your boundaries to protect, and then define the boundaries you need to protect what you treasure.

BLOCK THEM OUT OF YOUR LIFE

It might be tempting to share your success with your narcissist. For some, this desire may be fueled to show them that you are better than what they've said, while others may still feel that they want that person's approval. Regardless of your reason, don't. Once you've detached yourself, maintain that position and never resume contact.

YOU'LL EXPERIENCE DOUBT AND COMPLEX EMOTIONS—EMBRACE THEM

Some days may be good, and others much harder. Prepare yourself to go through a kaleidoscope of emotions; this experience is all part of the healing process. Embrace them all, for the harder you try to ignore negative emotions, the more persistent they'll become.

SPEND TIME WITH YOURSELF—DO THE THINGS YOU USED TO LOVE DOING

Make time for yourself. It is time to make your interests, passions, or simply relaxation a priority in your life. Schedule time to be with yourself; do the things you liked or liked in the past; and enjoy your own company, connecting with yourself.

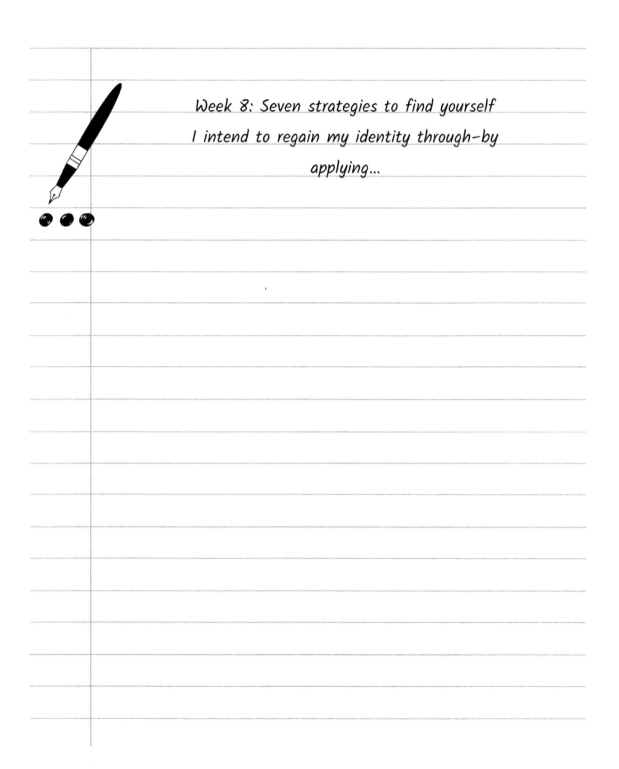

Week 8: Seven strategies to find yourself

I intend to regain my identity through–by

applying...

QUICK RECAP

- The term *identity* refers to a much more complex definition of who you are than what is widely understood.

- Identity forms and changes as time passes.

- Exposure to manipulation will impact your identity so severely that it can rob you of who you were

WEEK 9

HEALING BY CREATING TRUE AND LASTING RELATIONSHIPS

Social isolation has been a concept most people were unfamiliar with, at least until the global coronavirus (COVID-19) pandemic placed us all into lockdown. Yet, it is nothing new to the victims of gaslighters. Long before anyone knew the loneliness caused by the inability to connect to others, these victims experienced what it is like to live in isolation.

GASLIGHTING AND ISOLATION

Most of us tend to reach out to our support networks when we feel down, deflated, vulnerable, and uneasy in any uncomfortable situation we find ourselves in. When you are connected to a strong and supportive network, you gain the strength you seek from those who care about you during these times. This contact serves as a power injection when you need one the most, and while it is good for you, it goes entirely against the plans of the gaslighter.

In the wild, you'll find that predators would isolate one animal when they come across a group of animals they prey on. Once the animal is detached, pulling it down and completing the hunt with a kill becomes easier. Indeed this sounds like a harsh comparison, as being gaslighted is not the same as being killed, but let's focus on the modus operandi rather than the outcome. The gaslighter knows that as long as you have strong bonds you can draw on during your time of need, they'll struggle to gain complete control over you. So, gradually—and seemingly innocently—they will cause division between yourself and those you are connected to. The longer you stay in this relationship, the more depressed and stressed you become. Yet, as your ties with your network have been cut, you can only turn to the one person who has placed you in this position: your gaslighter. Thus, you continue to trust them, even if it is just because you have no other means to gain the emotional support and strength you need.

This entire situation plays into their hands as they can be both your hero and your villain, heightening your uncertainty whether they are genuinely as bad as you perceive them, for they are also good to you—albeit on their terms—when you need them. They may even pretend they turn to you for emotional support, helping them come across as vulnerable—they are not. It is all just part of their tactics to maintain control over you and to confuse your sense of reality. This is, of course, all impossible if you still have a network in place. Thus, the gaslighter will ensure that, gradually, all ties you have beyond this relationship are cut.

Week 9: Gaslighting and isolation

I felt isolated when...

THE ROLE HEALTHY RELATIONSHIPS PLAY IN OUR DEVELOPMENT

BUILDING BLOCKS IN OUR DEVELOPMENT

Sustained healthy and happy relationships are fundamental building blocks in our personal development and fulfill a vital role in especially sustaining our mental and emotional health and well-being. When we explore how these relationships contribute to our lives, it becomes evident why they are so vital and why the gaslighter is so precise in their attempts to stop their existence.

SUPPORTING US THROUGH CHALLENGING TIMES

Personal relationships offer us the support we need to get through challenging times and when facing hard choices. Within the safety of these relationships, we can express our deepest emotions and concerns and gain advice and insight from those who care about us.

THRIVE EMOTIONALLY

Loneliness has an immense impact on our emotional wellness, and it is often associated with depression and feelings of hopelessness. It is also closely linked to high suicide rates, especially during the festive season (Better Health Channel, 2022). People need human interaction and contact to thrive and even survive in life.

MAKE US HAPPY

When we have enough exposure to support and care through these relationships and bonds, we tend to be happier, be more content with life, and even live longer (Erryn, n.d.).

SECURE MENTAL STABILITY

Through these relationships, we learn how to better relate to other mentally stable and happy people and what healthy relationships should look like. They offer a benchmark to compare every other relationship you may have, including the one with your gaslighter. As it provides you with a fair and healthy comparison, these relationships will highlight the shortcomings and toxins in the relationship you have with the person abusing you in this manner, essentially blowing their cover and putting their efforts to a halt to avoid the risk of you ending the relationship.

BENEFITS OF HAVING HEALTHY RELATIONSHIPS

The list of benefits you'll be able to enjoy when you can sustain long-lasting and happy relationships is extensive. By experiencing these relationships or recalling a time when you had such relationships, you'll recognize the advantages you've appreciated. Nonetheless, the following three benefits are significant when you step out of a toxic relationship with a gaslighter, making it vital to form and strengthen such bonds.

Strong bonds increase your sense of purpose and provide you with direction. This is significant when you may feel lost from recently stepping out of a poisonous situation and needing to reclaim your life.

Through these bonds and observing what others are doing to sustain overall health and wellness, you gain insights into healthy behaviors and can adopt a new approach to taking care of yourself to improve your mental, physical, and emotional state. It can also be highly inspirational to observe others doing good for themselves, encouraging you to do the same.

Healthy relationships improve our self-esteem. For the longest time, your self-esteem has deliberately been destroyed to make you vulnerable and more likely to remain stuck in this toxic relationship. Through these relationships, you can improve your self-esteem, grow stronger, and find inspiration and motivation to continue living with purpose.

Week 9: Benefits of having healthy relationships

Healthy relationships would give me...

SIX STEPS YOU CAN TAKE TO IMPROVE YOUR PERSONAL RELATIONSHIPS

After being socially isolated for quite some time, it may be daunting to think about restoring past connections or establishing new ones. It may feel like you don't know where to start, and you may be concerned about whether people will accept you. The following steps will help to get you going on this quest.

DETERMINE YOUR NEEDS AND DEFINE THE NETWORK YOU NEED

For most of our lives, these relationships and the bonds we have with others are formed organically, meaning we hardly determine before forming these bonds what kind of people we would like to be connected to and actively seek out such people to include in our circle. Now you are going to do this, and you might as well seek a group that will complement your needs. So, before you form any bonds, determine the state of your self-esteem. Then, you need to decide who are the kind of people you would like to have relationships with and what you want to gain from these bonds. It may be that you are seeking empathy, support, or simply someone you can share your concerns with—or maybe you want to have fun and relax with your crowd:

- When you assess your self-esteem level, who are the people you are keen to have in your life?

- As you have the freedom to choose, create an avatar of the kind of person you want to reach out to and who will complement your needs for such a support group.

RESTORE EXISTING RELATIONSHIPS

It may be that not all your relationships are lost and that you still have bonds with others. These bonds may be neglected as you can't sustain them through regular contact. Evaluate these existing relationships in your life and see whether they are still valuable to you and whether you want to invest time in them to restore these bonds. Again, you would use your current state to determine what you would need. Since you are familiar with the people due to your existing bonds, you'll know which of these bonds you would want to restore and earmark the ones best left in a state of absence:

- Identify the relationship you want to restore in your life.

- What steps can you take immediately to begin the healing process?

WORK ON MANAGING YOUR EMOTIONS

Yes, you would like to form strong bonds with others because you would need people to be there for you, to support you, and to bring you joy. Nevertheless, you don't want to approach these relationships like you would with a support group. While you'll always be free and can benefit from being part of a support group, the most significant difference between a support group and friendship bonds is that it is not only about offering emotional support; it is a relationship of giving and taking. Just as you should be able to seek help from your relations, so should they be able to count on you for support when needed. Also, make sure that you have fun with these people, don't just turn every contact session into a time when you are downloading emotional baggage. Doing this will only be possible when you manage your emotions—at least to a certain degree.

BE OUT MORE OFTEN

Relationships take time to forge, and you have to invest effort and time into building these bonds. Therefore, bid your couch and binge-watch one series after another goodbye for a while as you step out more often to live your life and make memories with the people you are including in your support network. The more often you do this, the more confident you'll become:

- Draft a list of activities you would like to take part in. The list can include anything you are interested in and enjoy doing.

- Once you have the list, start doing the things that inspire you.

IDENTIFY YOUR EMOTIONAL BAGGAGE AND LET IT GO

The more emotional baggage you carry, the slower you progress to where you want to be. Friends will support you, but remember that empathy has an expiration date, and at some point, you need to let go of what is burdening you emotionally. Letting go of negative emotions would be even more vital when restoring existing relationships. In this case, letting go most likely means that you would have to forgive or ask to be forgiven:

- Do you have emotional baggage that is wearing you down?

- Are you ready to let this go?

- If not, what are you waiting for, and how long are you still willing to carry this burden?

CONTROL YOUR NEED TO JUMP TO CONCLUSIONS

While feeling vulnerable, it is easy to jump to conclusions, assuming that when someone is having an off day, it is because of something we said or did or that they don't like us. It is important to remember that the people we connect to are human too. They also experience days when they do not feel their best, meaning their behavior may have nothing to do with us. Rather than assuming the worst, understand that they might be struggling too and offer an ear willing to listen to their concerns.

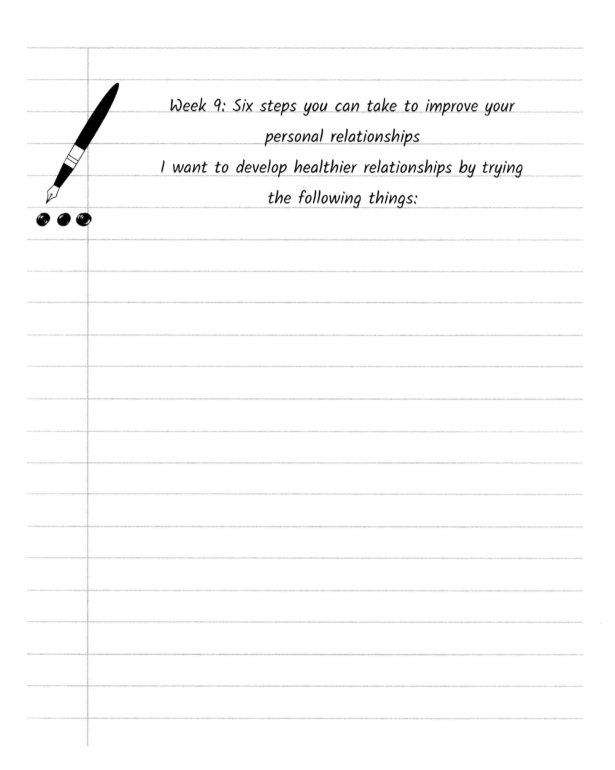

Week 9: Six steps you can take to improve your personal relationships

I want to develop healthier relationships by trying the following things:

PAMELA'S STORY

During her seven-year marriage, Pamela lost contact with her brother and sister. On separate occasions, her husband, John, had severe arguments with them, and they were no longer welcome in her home as her husband couldn't tolerate them. John's approach to her best friend, Sheila, was different. John would be around whenever Sheila visited, and after she had left, he would rip Sheila apart, stating how selfish or childish her behavior was and questioning how Pamela could be friends with someone so immature. Eventually, she also started to see less of Sheila. For about four years, John created a division between Pamela and everyone she was close to before they married. Thus, when Pamela finally left him, she was all alone.

While Pamela also decided to stick to having a few good friends around instead of having many acquaintances, she knew that she had to pick up the pieces of these relationships. She reached out to her sister, and they could restore their bond. She could also rebuild her friendship with Sheila, but her brother remains distant. Sometimes, we can fix broken relationships; we need to accept what happened and that we can't force people to forgive us. Then, it is best to move on while maintaining an open mind.

QUICK RECAP

- Gaslighters depend on social isolation to maintain their power position over you.

- People need social interaction with people with whom they are closely connected to be happy and content in life.

- Rebuilding or forging new relationships can be daunting, but there are many ways you can approach this venture with great success.

WEEK 10

HEALING BY CREATING YOUR OWN GOALS

To understand why the gaslighter wants you to let go of your goals, we need to know why gaslighters do what they do. According to Dr. Stephanie Sarkis, there are two reasons why gaslighters behave in this toxic manner: "'It is either a planned effort to gain control and power over another person, or it [is] because someone was raised by a parent or parents who were gaslighters, and they learned these behaviors as a survival mechanism'" (McQuillan, 2021, "Why Do People Gaslight?" para. 2).

Regardless of whether they do it for survival or to gain control—for the gaslight-tee—setting goals and pursuing what they want to achieve in life will disempower the gaslighter. When we follow our goals, we are committed to them and do what it takes to achieve them. It often also means that we are connected with a strong network and don't give the gaslighter all our time. Following your goals also requires structure and clarity in your life as well as being connected to reality. These are all things the gaslighter needs to be lacking in your life so that they can gain control. So, the victim's goals will directly conflict with the gaslighter's goals, and they will discourage you and create doubt and confusion. The gaslighter won't stop and is committed to doing what else it takes to get you off track of pursuing your dreams and goals. Thus, by design, we can say that the process of gaslighting demands that the victim doesn't have goals, as this would be in direct conflict with the process.

THE CONSEQUENCES OF LIVING WITHOUT GOALS

Some people have absolute clarity about what they want to achieve and know precisely how they will pursue their goals to succeed in their quest. A large part of the population would have vague goals. It means they may have an idea of what they want to achieve, but they have no set plans in place, and there is little clarity regarding how they want to do it. Some have no idea what goals they like to pursue, and for others, this is a natural state of being. However, for victims of a gaslighter, this is a forced state.

When observing what happens to someone robbed of all goals, it becomes clearer why the gaslighter doesn't want their victims to have any goals.

INCREASED FEAR OF FAILURE

The act of setting and pursuing goals comes with the risk of failure. You will have no certainty that you'll achieve what you set out to do. The best way to overcome this fear is to boost your confidence by setting smaller goals or breaking your goal down into milestones. Every time you achieve a milestone or a smaller goal, it increases your confidence in your ability to achieve what you want. Without this, your fear of failure only worsens and becomes overwhelming. It robs you of your independence and perfectly aligns with one of the most commonly used phrases of gaslighters: "You won't make it without me."

- Can you see how your lack of goals plays right into the hands of a gaslighter?

AN INCREASED SENSE OF BEING OVERWHELMED

As long as we are in a state of feeling overwhelmed, we lack clarity in our vision. The lack of clarity distorts our perception of reality. This is, of course, also beneficial to the gaslighter as the more your perception of reality is distorted, the easier it becomes to remove you from it.

AN INCREASED SENSE OF REJECTION

While pursuing our goals, we are facing repeated rejection. It is just part of the process. The more you knock on doors to progress, the greater the odds of having doors closed in your face. The more often you do it, the more you become comfortable with the idea that sometimes you'll face rejection and other times you won't. You become at ease with being rejected. Yet, when you lack the opportunities to be denied and to grow more comfortable with it, the more you fear the unknown, making the idea of rejection much worse than what it truly is. As the fear of rejection becomes such a significant concept in your mind, it is easy for the gaslighter to convince you that you'll always be rejected, even in places or people where this is not the case. Your fear or rejection becomes a vital tool contributing to the gaslighter's attempts to isolate and remove you from your support networks.

Week 10: The consequences of living without goals

Living without goals, I learned that...

KELSEY'S STORY

Kelsey had big dreams when she met Pete. She wanted to start her own business. She had clarity on what she wanted to do with her life, which was aligned with the purpose she believed was hers and with which she felt comfortable. Her goals were big but achievable as she believed in herself. While she was convinced that Pete had her back, as he would be supportive when it didn't really matter, he was sinking her confidence in her ability every time she faced failure. When a client cancels a contract, Pete would tell her that she needs to understand that her product may not be as good as she thought it would be. He would shift her focus to all that could go wrong in her business and how it would fail under the pretense that he was only playing devil's advocate as he loved her and wanted her to be prepared for anything. Yet, when she had some success, he would barely acknowledge it; when she would fail, he would tell her that it was just confirmation of how he was right by preparing her for failure.

Eventually, exposure to this constant negativity and doubt in her ability to achieve her goals worked on Kelsey's mindset, and her confidence in her ability to achieve her dreams was shredded. As her business was her only income, she began to make business choices out of fear rather than confidence. As her business deteriorated, Pete would swoop in and tell her that he was there for her and would always support her, but when they had an argument, he reminded her that he takes care of her and that she is nothing without him. This crippled Kelsey's confidence, and she entirely depended on Pete, giving him complete control over her life.

WHY YOU NEED TO SET GOALS

Setting clear goals is beneficial during any stage of life or under any circumstances. There are certain benefits to goal setting that can be especially helpful in your recovery and healing after being in a relationship with a gaslighter.

GOALS GIVE YOU DIRECTION

One of the most common concerns I've noticed with victims of gaslighters is that they have no direction. The lack of knowing what they want to do or what they should do next becomes increasingly stressful as time goes by. Goal setting can come in handy in these types of situations.

"Goals give you direction, purpose, and a destination to reach. Goals motivate you to take action and provide a clear roadmap and path to follow each day toward goal achievement" (Pettit, 2020, "10 Benefits of Goal Setting," para. 2). When you set goals and draft a plan to achieve what you've set out to do, you have clear instructions to follow, making progress possible even when you have no idea what you should do next.

GOALS INCREASE YOUR CLARITY

Setting goals demands a clear understanding of what you want and how you will get there. By becoming active in goal setting, you are forcing yourself to shift your focus away from your current circumstances and emotional state toward what you want and where you want to be. It is a conscious decision to let go of the confusion you may be trapped in and anchor yourself outside your whirlpool of emotions. Finding this clarity is a significant achievement on your road to recovery.

GOALS OFFER CONTROL

When you've set your goals, you must determine where you are heading and how you want to get there. This puts you back in control of your life as you'll be steering your future and determining the direction you are heading in. The full rein you gain through goal setting is empowering and will increase your confidence and self-esteem.

SEVEN STEPS TO GOAL-SETTING SUCCESS

The first step to success is the most challenging step to take. After that, it goes much easier, and you'll soon find momentum when you keep going. The same is true when it comes to goal setting. The following seven steps will help you to gain momentum and find your rhythm in the process.

DEFINE THE END AT THE BEGINNING

Before setting any goals, define what outcome you would like, as there are many ways you can achieve the same results. It is not always as important how you achieve the desired outcome, but what is important is that you do achieve it.

For example, let's say you seek a future where you can enjoy financial freedom. You define financial freedom as having the choice to determine your working hours and where you would like to work from and still be financially independent. Once you have clarity on this, you can explore the different ways you'll be able to achieve this outcome. Some options may be starting an online retail store, finding a remote position offering a salary that will satisfy your needs, or even venturing into several passive income opportunities. It would help if you determined which of these options complements your identity the best:

- What is the outcome you are looking for?

- Once you've listed all the requirements you want your goals to meet, create another list of possible opportunities to deliver these results.

CONFIRM YOUR GOAL

When you've decided on what you need to do, confirm your goal by writing it down. Share your ideas with someone you trust, as this person will become your soundboard to bounce off your thoughts and keep you accountable to stick to your plans. Having someone who will keep you accountable can be a great aid when you feel weak and are ready to give up:

- Identify the person you want to have as your soundboard and accountability partner.

- Share your goals with the person you've identified.

PLAN YOUR GOAL

Goals should be significant. However, big goals are hard to reach; therefore, you need to break your goal down into smaller, achievable milestones. Your plan should include every step of every milestone. You have to clearly define your milestones, determine how you will measure your progress, set timelines for achieving these goals, and decide how to reward yourself every time you reach a milestone:

- Explore your goal and see how you can break it into smaller segments.

- SMART goals are goals that meet the following traits: specific, measurable, achievable, relevant, and time-bound.

- Take every segment or milestone and transform them into SMART goals in their own rights.

For example, when the big goal is to start an online store, a milestone would be to design your website. To be specific, you'll state that you have to get your website platform designed. You can measure your progress by determining how far along you are, and once your platform is live, you'll know you've accomplished this step. As many service providers can help you, and others have done it many times, it is achievable. It is relevant to your goal, and you only need to determine when you want it done.

CONTINUE YOUR PROGRESS

As milestones are smaller steps to take, you'll be able to continue your progress as you've set sustainable actions for yourself. When you struggle to maintain momentum, turn to the person you've entrusted to keep you accountable. It can be frustrating when you don't see the results you are hoping for as quickly as you want but keep reminding yourself that progress is better than perfection.

CELEBRATE EVERY ACHIEVEMENT

Regardless of your achievement's size, be sure to celebrate it, for every celebration gives your confidence in your ability the boost it needs to continue progress. Determining how you will celebrate your achievements when you draft your plan is essential. These celebrations don't have to be lavish. Instead, think in line with things you enjoy but seldom have a chance to do: reading a book or taking a long bath, or having coffee and cake with a friend. These are rewards you can use to make achieving your goals even more fun, give you something to look forward to, and establish balance in your life so that it is not only about work all the time:

- What would you like to reward yourself with to celebrate achieving your milestones?

START LIVING

For far too long, you may have been living a limited life without the freedom you deserve to achieve your dreams. Setting goals is not only about completing a to-do list to keep you busy for the rest of your life. No, the primary purpose of goal setting is to create the life you desire so that you can start living:

- Are you ready to take up the reins to steer your life in the direction you desire so that you can start living life again?

Week 10: Start living

When meeting my goals, I'll feel...

QUICK RECAP

- Gaslighters don't like their victims to have goals, as the victim's commitment to their goals directly conflicts with what the gaslighter wants to achieve.

- Without goals, we become lost, feel rejected, lose focus, and are merely drifting.

- Goal setting has many benefits; some can be especially helpful on your journey.

- Goal setting can be easy when you follow a few simple steps.

WEEK 11

10 PRACTICAL WAYS TO REGAIN YOUR SANITY AFTER YOU'VE BEEN GASLIGHTED

While a large part of healing would constitute self-reflection and taking time to explore and identify your emotions and thoughts, there is also a practical aspect to it that you must complete ensuring your desired progress. In this chapter, I am equipping you with 10 practical steps to help you regain your sanity, become empowered, and confidently take on the position at the helm of your life.

STEP 1—SCRAPE CLOSURE OFF YOUR TO-DO LIST

Closure is often an essential part of healing, and it is common for people to seek closure after suffering a severe loss before they can progress. It may be that you feel that after having distance between you and your gaslighter for some time, you would like to meet up again and discuss what happened so that you can get closure too. This won't be possible when you are recovering from gaslighting. Gaslighters are, by nature, just not the kind of people with whom you can have a relationship postmortem and walk away with greater clarity; they can't have a conversation without pushing an agenda to get you back into their control. Do you really want to risk falling back into this trap? Rather, accept that there are certain things you can't control, and a gaslighter's approach is one of those things. Yet, you have control over letting go of this desire for your own good. Make that distinction and work on finding peace that it is the way it is:

- Writing a letter to your ex to tell them precisely what you feel and think, sharing all you usually do during closure, can be beneficial. It is a way to unburden your mind and let go of the things holding you back. Once you are done, burn the letter as a gesture to set yourself free emotionally.

Week 11: Step 1

Dear...

STEP 2—TAKE TIME TO GRIEF

While you can't find closure, you can grieve over the loss you've suffered. This person may not have been good for you, but it doesn't mean that you didn't have beautiful dreams for your future. You've invested in yourself and tried to make it work for as long as you've been in this relationship. You were sincerely committed to a dream. Now, you find yourself in a situation similar to depositing money into a savings account, and when you want to withdraw, you learn that it is empty. You've suffered a loss in the sense of your time; a part of your life; your dreams and hopes for the relationship; and who you were before it all started. It is perfectly fine to mourn these losses. Allow yourself permission to grieve and know that it doesn't mean you want the person back in your life. Just be alert of getting trapped in the mourning stage as you need to move and start living again:

- People grieve in different ways. Define how you would prefer to grieve and set time apart for active grieving. For example, go away for a weekend to a place where you can spend time in a neutral environment to process your emotions and say goodbye to all you've lost.

Week 11: Step 2

I need to mourn...

STEP 3—FIND FORGIVENESS FOR YOURSELF

We can be very hard on ourselves. Many possible questions can consume your mind, varying from how you could be so stupid, to why you didn't see the signs earlier. Feeling embarrassed by what happened to you is expected, as you may think you've allowed it to happen.

Stop! You are a survivor of deep emotional and mental manipulation applied by someone highly skilled and driven to gain control over you. Your sincere desire to make the relationship work and to be the best partner to this person you can be, trusting they desired the same, gave them an unfair advantage in a contest you didn't sign up for. Be kind to yourself and forgive yourself. Forgiving yourself doesn't equate to thinking of yourself as a victim; think of yourself as a survivor:

- List the challenges you were facing and what you've overcome along the way. Celebrate these achievements by doing something good for yourself.

Week 11: Step 3

I forgive myself because...

STEP 4—LEARN AS MUCH AS POSSIBLE

Knowledge empowers us. By learning as much as you can about narcissism and gaslighting, you'll better understand how gaslighters operate, why they do it, and how they manage to trap you. Afterward, you'll feel more empowered. By expanding your knowledge base in this regard, you may even notice that you were the stronger one for getting away. You are on a quest to improve and develop yourself and to show personal growth, whereas the gaslighter will likely remain stuck in the same position:

- This book offers a great foundation to familiarize yourself with gaslighting and what it entails, but there is also a wealth of information you can tap into to expand your knowledge further. Feel free to read more on the topic.

STEP 5—GATHER AN EMOTIONAL SUPPORT KIT

Recovery is a journey with many ups and downs. There will be days when you feel on top of the world—or as close to it as you've been in a long time. There will also be days when you are in the deepest and darkest pools of negativity. When you are experiencing these challenging days, acknowledge it for what it is: part of your recovery.

Gather what you need in your emotional support kit during the good days. These would be things that leave you feeling better. As the dark days can be so challenging that you can't even remember the things that make you feel better, it is best to keep a list of things you can do to lift your mood. This can be reading a good book—make sure you have one within reach—taking a walk in nature, spending time with animals at a shelter, or volunteering your services to distract your focus. List these things and keep whatever you need to use the list on hand:

- Draft a list of the things you can do that are easy to access and affordable so as to make you feel better.

- Keep the list on the fridge or where you can find it easily on the days you need your support kit.

STEP 6—MAKE A POSITIVE MIND SHIFT

People are naturally inclined to lean towards the negative. We can ponder on the worst possible outcomes in life. We do this knowing that good and bad outcomes both have a fifty-fifty chance of realizing. Due to our natural leniency towards negativity, the brain develops strong and established neuron pathways conveying negative impulses. Yet, you can change the neuron network in your brain by deliberately choosing positivity.

Establish positive neuron paths by constantly shifting your thoughts from negative to positive. You can even picture how you create new pathways in your brain while taking your daily walk. Every step establishes these paths, eventually leading you away from pondering on all the emotional abuse you've suffered during your relationship:

- Are you taking regular strolls? Transform these exercise sessions into meditative walks, visualizing how you use every step to change the neuron pathways in your mind.

STEP 7—DON'T COMPARE YOURSELF

It is best to cut all contact with your gaslighter, but sometimes a friend or relative may give you the inside scoop as they might have seen your ex with their new partner. Again, curiosity can sometimes take the driving seat, and you may want to take a peek to see for yourself with whom they've replaced you. You know you shouldn't, but still, you do. When you do, the temptation may be overwhelming to compare yourself with that person physically and on other levels. Before you do, remember that person has no idea what they are in for. You also had a unique radiance before you stepped into a relationship with your gaslighter, and while they may have taken that from you, you survived and broke free from the abuse. Rather than feeling inferior, jealous, or hurt by looking at the person, feel sincere empathy for them. They likely have no idea what kind of relationship they are stepping into:

- Rather than comparing yourself, draft a list of things you would say to the version of you getting into a relationship with a gaslighter when you were in your ex's new partner's position.

STEP 8—DON'T MEDDLE IN THEIR NEW RELATIONSHIP

Since you feel empathy for the new person in your ex's life, you want to tell them what they are in for. You want to warn them, and there are two reasons you want to do it. The first reason is that you feel sorry for them and are genuinely concerned about the emotional well-being of the new person. You don't want them to suffer through the same relationship as you did. The second reason is that you want to show your ex that you have control too. You want to make a point and to see them crash and burn.

Please don't do it. First, they'll never believe you, as your gaslighter has already painted a picture of you being completely out of touch with reality and an emotionally unstable wildcard. Now you show up and warn their new partner, someone who can only see the good in this person, and you'll come across as the crazy person your ex has made you out to be.

Even if they listen to your advice and break it off with your ex, they will only go out and find new "supplies" to manipulate. Doing so will hinder your recovery, and you've wasted enough time and energy on this person. Now is your time to focus on yourself and allow the other person to walk their journey in life without you meddling in their business:

- Sometimes the best course of action we can take is actually inaction. Make it your motto in this regard. What happens in your ex's life is not your business and is no longer part of your journey. Instead, maintain your focus on your growth and progress.

STEP 9—STOP PONDERING ABOUT WHAT HAPPENED

It can be easy to immerse yourself in thoughts, questioning what happened. By staying immersed in these thoughts and wondering what happened, what caused the outcome, and what you did wrong, you are only halting your progress. Remind yourself that you are the only one doing it. Not for one day will a gaslighter ponder on the past and explore what they've done wrong, for they didn't do anything wrong in their eyes. Yes, they may present themselves as victims who only wanted to do good, but remember that the gaslighter may at times return when they don't get their way with another. Therefore, they will try their luck again with you, so they have to keep the doorway paved with sympathy open to you.

Save yourself the agony of thinking that they are missing you or are hurt by you. This advice comes with the warning that it may be highly challenging to do this as it is not in your good nature to treat people like this, but it was your good nature that the gaslighter took advantage of in the first place:

- Find alternative places to express your good nature and be kind to others. Maybe explore what volunteering options are in your vicinity and get involved in such an initiative.

STEP 10—MAKE CHOICES OF YOUR OWN

After breaking free from the toxic relationship, you may be taken aback by how long it takes to make choices for your own benefit. One would think that it would be the first thing you would want to do after being trapped in a relationship where you were disempowered and controlled by your partner, yet you didn't. If you are going to extensively postpone making choices that will benefit you, it may become hard to make these choices. Thus, as part of your recovery and to speed up healing, make a choice purely for your benefit. It can be something minor, like ordering food from a restaurant that your ex didn't like or going on a trip to a place you wouldn't have been able to go to otherwise. It doesn't matter what you choose—make that choice yourself to benefit you:

- What choice are you making today to benefit you?

QUICK RECAP

- Recovery would include emotional healing through introspection as it will help you to come to terms with your emotions and thoughts.

- Yet, there are also several practical steps you can take to help your progress.

WEEK 12

HEALING BY MASTERING YOUR MOTIVATION

Antonio nervously walked into the therapy room and immediately started to shout loudly and decisively, "Sir, you can tell me anything, but I will never give up on what I am doing." He was using ethnobotanicals and sought happiness in them. He had no intention of giving up on his old life. After all, why would he choose a different path after fate had just offered him an opportunity to feel better? Why would he choose a less burdensome route if he was already walking a path full of excitement and unsuspected *options*? His gaze was lost and empty. He truly was a prisoner of his own past. He was sad and lacking motivation, and he had lost all hope that things could ever turn out differently.

WHAT IS THE ALTERNATIVE?

It was the first exploratory question I brought up. Sit down at the table of honesty. Propagate the following scenario into your mind: Let's assume that you will do absolutely nothing about your past. You will let the trauma, pain, misery, and abuse go on and manifest. You won't bother having a well-balanced relationship with yourself or those around you. You won't do anything about your present either. You will strangle the pain and sorrow every time they make their presence felt. You will not accept the things that cannot be changed and you will not forgive what needs to be forgiven. You will take no interest in your emotions or thoughts. You will not be bothered by all the sores, affronts, and wounds carved into your soul. And so, you will proceed in the exact same manner as you did before. The question that comes up to mind sounds like this: *What is the alternative?*

Allow me to make things easier for you. The alternative is terrible. A future full of pain and horrible events. Lack of confidence and loss of identity. Crippling toward life's struggles. In simpler words, you will never be able to do any different than what you've already done so far. You will be living day in and day out bearing the same whipping thoughts and realities. So, before you try changing something, answer these questions truthfully: If I don't make a change, then where will everything lead to? What would be the consequences of living in the same way through the end?

Week 12: What is the alternative?

Let your thoughts come to you. Be gentle to yourself, but examine everything with honesty. Write down everything that comes to mind at the moment. Come back when you feel more prepared!

HOW MOTIVATED AM I RIGHT NOW?

Susan Fowler has introduced a transformative idea that I intend to convey as close to the reader's mind as possible: "Motivation is at the heart of everything you do and everything you don't do but wish you did."

Before you start improving yourself, you need to have a closer look at what I call the motivation thermometer. What do I mean when I say a motivation thermometer? Sit back down at the table of honesty. Try to look deep inside yourself and quantify what you really wish for. Assess the intensity of your motivation. On a scale of 1–10, how badly do you wish you could change what is bugging you? Remember the example that I used at the beginning of this chapter? Antonio's motivation was bluntly stated: no motivation whatsoever.

Supposing you have come to an honest conclusion. Ask yourself, why did you score the way you did? If you have a score of 6, what makes you rate it that way? What are the main factors that lead to such a high level of motivation?

Let's say you wish to increase your level of motivation from 6 to 8. What would have to change in order to achieve such an output? Who could possibly kick-start what needs to happen in order to get you where you want to be?

HOW IMPORTANT IS THIS TO ME?

Being a therapist, I often encounter two main reasons why people are willing to truly change. The first one is called grief. The human body and mind do not accommodate pain very well. It's the reason that prompts us to visit the doctor's office. It's what drives us to shy away from potentially destructive experiences. All the pain lingering within us is conveying a message. In other words, the pain is not rooted inside us by chance. This pain gently whispers, "You need to stop now. You've barely survived up to this point, and now it no longer serves you to continue in the same way as before." Have another seat at the table of honesty. Spend some time with your pain, don't constrict it and don't try to make it stop. Discover its message and accept it. The pain is there; you can embrace it, and turn it into a trigger for change. Most of the time, the pain sinks in with an incredibly clear and profound message: *I want you to change; I wish you wouldn't suffer so much. I wish you would be stronger and escape the chains of the past.*

So, turn your pain into your companion. Listen to its message, understand it, and be inspired. This is how true motivation is created! Looking in with tear-stained eyes at our inner pain.

The other reason why people change is called importance. How important is it for you to change? Sit down again at the table of honesty and let the following scenario play out in your mind! When there is no meaningful reason, there is no real change. Think of all the changes you would like to take effect. If they were really important to you, what would you do about them? Importance often determines success. How could you love something that isn't important enough to you? How could you put substantial effort into something that's not worth it?

It's time to figure out the importance you give when it comes to doing the things you want to do. Likewise, if you come to the conclusion that change is not important to you, don't beat yourself up too much. Ask yourself, Why isn't it important? When did it start to become less important? Under what circumstances would you begin to feel that it is really important to work on yourself?"

Your mind is important. Your thoughts are important. Your emotions are important. The decisions you make right now are important. Your reputation is important. Your story is important. Some of it has already been written without your consent, but things are far from being over. The other bits and pieces are up to you. Don't let what is already written determine the ending. You can still write down what you wish to be kept! Strive to refocus your mind on what's significant to you, and once you've determined what really matters, your heart and spirit will begin to fight harder and harder in order to create new standards. Take your time, work on understanding the importance of your goals, and then the fuel of motivation will start to kick in.

Week 12: How important is this to me?

What is the message of my pain?

POWERFUL WAYS TO INCREASE SELF-MOTIVATION

1. IDENTIFY THE BELIEFS THAT ARE HINDERING YOUR MOTIVATION

The main issues which come as a result of gaslight abuse have to do with our internalized beliefs, perspectives, and projections about ourselves. For example, we may have been repeatedly and abusively told that we are worthless. And so, the odds are high that we consider ourselves dumb and useless. Maybe deep down we feel that we are not capable of doing anything right and that we destroy everything we touch. It is nearly impossible to act in contradiction with the way we perceive ourselves to be. It is nearly impossible to motivate someone whom I believe to be stupid, incapable, irredeemable, and beyond salvation.

When the internalized convictions and projections you have about yourself are destructive and malevolent, there is no motivation left. Thus, we can rarely rise above what we believe ourselves to be. The fruit of a tree cannot be growing well if there are serious issues at the root. Therefore, it is fundamental to confront all your thoughts regarding yourself. What have you come to believe to be true about what you've been told you are? When you come across a challenge that is stronger than you, what are the first thoughts that cross your mind? Going further and analyzing in detail, what impact does it have on you? What is it that drives you to see it through?

Once you have succeeded in becoming aware and figuring out what assumptions you have about yourself, it is essential to move on to what we call counteracting. There are many different ways of challenging the beliefs we hold about ourselves and rebranding them into something different. Look at the evidence. What evidence is there to show that you might be stupid? Are there data that suggest otherwise? What do these things say about you? If you have failed in some of life's pursuits, is it fair to label yourself as eternally worthless? How useful is it to apply a life sentence to yourself? How do other people perceive you?

Week 12: Identify the beliefs that are hindering

your motivation

2. DREAM

Such abuse is gruesome, inhumane, and cruel, and it takes an enormous toll on the human psyche. What I am trying to say is that it absolutely shatters the wings that can pull us up. It leaves no space for you and your own dreams. It prohibits our dreams and our growth potential. When there are no dreams for us to seek out, there is no motivation. Perhaps in some ways, I am asking you to do the most courageous thing you have ever done. To dream! Let your mind unfold what you really aspire to achieve. Out of the tens of thousands of lives you could be living, which one do you dream about the most? What are the places you've always wanted to visit? Suppose you had the ability to work anywhere you'd like; what would you decide to do?

Dream in such a way that the walls of your heart hit your chest really hard. Only then will you know you're dreaming properly. Dream about the major dimensions of your life. Dream about your emotional life. What do you want it to look like? Dream about the romantic and family aspects. What would you wish would happen there? Dream about your ideal professional life. What does the dream show you? Dream about fulfillment and meaning in life. What is the voice of your fulfillment? How is your life meaning projected to you? Dream about decision-making. Suppose you were making some decisions that would define the story of your life and the lives of those who will come after you. What do you think those decisions would be? The incentive is simple: Don't stop dreaming!

Week 12: Dream

3. FROM DREAM TO REALITY

We saw first-hand the importance of dealing with our own beliefs about ourselves. Then we crystallized the importance of our dreams. Now we need to move from dreaming to setting a factual and intelligent enough goal. Suppose you dream of having more confidence in your abilities. This is a dream that falls into the emotional sphere. There is a vast difference between dreaming to become confident and aiming to achieve it in the truest sense of the word. *I aim to have more confidence in myself.*

Define your goal: How much time will it take you to achieve what you set out to achieve? Half a year, one full year, two years, how long will you work on this assignment?

When precisely will you know that the goal has been achieved? How will you know that this is really the case?

What are the resources that you have at hand in order to achieve this goal? And what about the setbacks? What might stop you from succeeding?

Think concisely and factually, and don't philosophize too much. How are you going to do it? Through what kind of actions and experiences? What are the actions that will contribute to achieving your goal? What do you intend to do this week–month?

The idea is simple: The more specific the plan is, the greater the chances of success.

4. DON'T FORGET YOUR COMRADES

There will be great times in your life when you will be motivated from within to do whatever it is you want. In other words, you'll have all the confidence, determination, and reasoning in the palm of your hand. You will have a powerful sense of the meaning of what you want to do. You will truly believe in your recovery and take the necessary steps in order to succeed on your own. Enjoy experiencing and relishing.

On the other hand, life can often be regarded as a long journey where you are constantly rowing to get to where you want to be. Sometimes you will get tired, and you will not be able to row, which means that your motivation will be severely impacted. You won't be able to find your own reasoning, and you will lack the confidence you need. You'll be disappointed and despondent, and at some point, you'll drop the rowing. In other words, you will be tempted to stop moving forward altogether. Those are moments when you will have to rely on other people to help you get through the tough times. From time to time, you'll get sick, injured, or unable to function at 100% capacity. You'll often feel exhausted after desperate attempts and trials to recover. In those moments, your comrades–friends–mentors will jump to your aid in order to help you move forward. They will give of their strength so that you can gain more. They will watch over you and check up on you. They will be able to help you find the determination and the reasoning needed to move forward. Their support will probably save your life. You will be forever transformed.

Take a very careful and patient glance around you while trying to pinpoint who your comrades are. Some will turn out to be a less fortunate choice, but others will row alongside you. It will be extremely difficult or almost impossible to succeed without their support and care. Let them support you and be there for you. Hold on to them and share vulnerable situations with them. You will then find another source of motivation that is not possible to achieve in other circumstances.

5. DON'T GIVE UP!

You'll be subjected to challenges like never before. You'll probably be mercilessly tormented. You will be disgraced in front of other people. You will fail enough times that the doubt will be outright and overwhelming. You will weep many times, and there will be pain. Lots and lots of it. There will always be ways out, but the outcome will be disastrous. Forget about getting it together, and you won't have to worry for a while. Things will be business as usual. You'll get rid of hard work and painful memories. You'll avoid pain and suffering for a while, but let me tell you something...

If you give up now, you'll regret it for the rest of your life. If you give up now, things will not get any better. By doing so, you will always live with the uncertainty of not knowing how great you really could've been. You'll never be able to see how things could've changed for you. The pain is temporary, but the regret will last forever. I've never met a case in therapy that has challenged this reality.

Lastly, I want you to know that every single effort you put in will have a unique resonance in your life! Simultaneously, I guarantee you that it won't be easy, yet I trust that the resources you have been given here will help you implement changes and gain insights that you will truly value. It is a great honor for me to know that my readers are out there, benefiting from the engagement and thoughts conveyed through my work. Have faith in your healing process! Good luck with everything, God bless you!

Week 12: Congratulations! You've put in a lot of

hard and valuable work!

Keep on applying everything you've learned so far!

Seek to learn beyond what you already know!

Enjoy the journey you are on and the one that lies

ahead! Take care of yourself!

CONCLUSION

The most accurate way to summarize *gaslighting* is to refer to it as an abuse of your sanity. It is a well-calculated approach to rob you of your perception of reality, make you doubt your perceptions, isolate you from any anchors keeping you linked to actuality, and prey on your vulnerabilities to maintain control over your actions and power over your life. Licensed psychoanalyst and cofounder of the Yale Center for Emotional Intelligence Dr. Robin Stern explains gaslighting as follows: "When a loved one undermines your sense of reality, you become trapped in this never-never land... You feel crazy because there isn't anything concrete to point to as 'bad,' so you end up pointing to, and blaming, yourself" (Andersen, 2020, para. 3).

Gaslighting can occur in any relationship, including parental bonds, at the workplace, and between friends. However, it is most prevalent in romantic relationships, where women are more often the victims of gaslighting than men. The Centre for Disease Control and Prevention estimates that 43 million women and 38 million men are victims of emotional abuse from a romantic partner (Andersen, 2020).

I am presenting these statistics here, at the end of the book, because if there is one realization that I want to settle with you, it is the fact that you are not alone in this challenging position. What I want to add onto this idea is that you are not at fault here. You trusted someone, and they took advantage of your good nature.

Yet, you are a survivor. You have or can break free from this abuse, and you can rebuild your life, connect with your identity, and set goals to fulfill your purpose.

Throughout the past 12 weeks, we've explored how you can regain control over your emotions, and we've invested our time in exploring ways to define your reality. This refers to your reality, not the one the gaslighter wanted you to perceive as real. You've become a master at controlling your thoughts, enabling you to make decisions for yourself again. The only way to break free from a life with a gaslighter and the aftermath of being with someone abusing you mentally and emotionally is to detach and remain detached—even when some time has passed.

Now, you can find your identity, rebuild your support network, set goals for your future and start living the way intended for you. You can do this, knowing you are stronger than you think and can overcome obstacles. As you are a survivor, you can confidently and courageously live freely.

PS: Thank you for taking the time to read *The Gaslighting & Narcissistic Abuse Recovery Workbook.*

I hope you've enjoyed the journey.

I'm confident that the advice and activity boxes found in this book will help you start living the life you truly deserve.

I have a favor to ask you. If something in this book resonated with you, would you please take a moment and leave a review on Amazon? Reviews may not matter to public figures but it does matter for little guys like myself. They encourage other folks to read my content.

Scan the QR Code to leave your honest feedback.

OTHER BOOKS WRITTEN BY ANDREI NEDELCU

The Codependency Recovery Workbook: A12-Week Master Plan to Stop Being Codependent and Start Loving Yourself

Scan the QR code to check it out

Facing and Overcoming Codependency: Practical Guidance to Fix Your Codependency, Stop Being a People Pleaser, and Start Loving Yourself

Scan the QR code to check it out

Facing and Overcoming Codependency: From Being Needy & Clingy to Having Amazing, Authentic, and Loving Relationships

Scan the QR code to check it out

REFERENCES

Andersen, C. H. (2020, November 17). *16 gaslighting phrases that are red flags.* The Healthy. https://www.thehealthy.com/family/relationships/gaslighting-phrases/

Arzt, N. (2022, November 24). *20 examples of gaslighting: Relationships, parents, friends, & coworkers.* Choosing Therapy. https://www.choosingtherapy.com/examples-of-gaslighting/

Better Health Channel. (2022, February 24). *Strong relationships, strong health.* Department of Health, State Government of Victoria, Australia. https://www.betterhealth.vic.gov.au/health/HealthyLiving/Strong-relationships-strong-health

Brockway, L. H. (2020, December 31). *24 phrases "gaslighters" use against you.* PR Daily. https://www.prdaily.com/24-phrases-gaslighters-use-against-you/

Caporuscio, J. (2020, May 13). *How does isolation affect mental health?* Medical News Today. https://www.medicalnewstoday.com/articles/isolation-and-mental-health#who-is-at-risk

Cleveland Clinic. (n.d.). *Narcissistic personality disorder.* https://my.clevelandclinic.org/health/diseases/9742-narcissistic-personality-disorder#:~:text=Experts%20estimate%20that%20up%20to

Decision Making. (n.d.). SkillsYouNeed. https://www.skillsyouneed.com/ips/decision-making.html

Delagran, L. (n.d.). *Impact of fear and anxiety.* University of Minnesota. https://www.takingcharge.csh.umn.edu/impact-fear-and-anxiety

Dimitrijevic, I. (n.d.). *25 tips to help you improve any relationship in your life.* Lifehack. https://www.lifehack.org/articles/communication/tips-help-you-improve-any-relationship-your-life.html

Dohms, E. (2018, October 29). *Gaslighting makes victims question reality.* Wisconsin Public Radio. https://www.wpr.org/gaslighting-makes-victims-question-reality

Erryn. (n.d.). *Gaslighting and social isolation: An intertwined tale as old as time.* Broader Lines. http://broaderlines.com/gaslighting-and-social-isolation-a-binding%E2%80%8B-tale-as-old-as-time/

Ghita, C. (n.d.). *10 steps to improve your personal relationships.* Lifehack. https://www.lifehack.org/articles/communication/10-steps-improve-your-personal-relationships.html

Gordon, S. (2022, November 7). *What is gaslighting?* Verywell Mind. https://www.verywellmind.com/is-someone-gaslighting-you-4147470

Identity. (n.d.). Psychology Today. https://www.psychologytoday.com/za/basics/identity

Johnson, M. Z. (2016, March 28). *6 unexpected ways I've healed from gaslighting abuse and learned to trust myself again.* Everyday Feminism. https://everydayfeminism.com/2016/03/healed-from-gaslighting-abuse/

Lincoln, C. (2022, November 24). *25 gaslighting phrases abusers use.* Choosing Therapy. https://www.choosingtherapy.com/gaslighting-phrases/

McQuillan, S. (2021, November 2). *Gaslighting: What is it and why do people do it?* Psycom. https://www.psycom.net/gaslighting-what-is-it

Nall, R. (2020, June 29). *What are the long-term effects of gaslighting?* Medical News Today. https://www.medicalnewstoday.com/articles/long-term-effects-of-gaslighting

Narcissistic personality disorder. (2021, December 27). PsychDB. https://www.psychdb.com/personality/narcissistic#:~:text=DSM%2D5%20 Diagnostic%20 Criteria Text=Is%20preoccupied%20with%20fantasies%20of

No motivation, no goals, no dreams = An undeniable nothing. (2022, November 29). Wiedel on Winning. https://weidelonwinning.com/blog/no-motivation-no-goals-no-dreams-an-undeniable-nothing/

Northpoint Recovery. (2022, May 23). *Gaslighting: Examples, effects and how to confront the abuse.* https://www.northpointrecovery.com/blog/gaslighting-examples-effects-confront-abuse/

Northwestern Medicine. (2021, September). *5 benefits of healthy relationships.* https://www.nm.org/healthbeat/healthy-tips/5-benefits-of-healthy-relationships

Pettit, M. (2020, September 16). *10 crucial benefits of goal setting.* Lucemi Consulting. https://lucemiconsulting.co.uk/benefits-of-goal-setting/#:~:text=The%20benefits%20of%20setting%20goals

A quote by Robin Sharma. (n.d.). Books Ameya. https://booksameya.in/everything-is-created-twice-first-in-the-mind-and-then-in-reality/#:~:text=Robin%20Sharma%20is%20a%20Canadian

Raypole, C. (2020, April 28). *How to become the boss of your emotions.* Healthline. https://www.healthline.com/health/how-to-control-your-emotions

Rice, M. (2022, February 7). *What is narcissistic gaslighting?* Talkspace. https://www.talkspace.com/mental-health/conditions/articles/narcissistic-gas-lighting/#:~:text=Gaslighting%20is%20the%20use%20of

Saeed, K. (n.d.). *Healing from identity loss after narcissistic abuse.* Kim Saeed. https://kimsaeed.com/2018/07/08/healing-from-identity-loss/

Sarkis, S. (2018, October 4). *This is why victims of gaslighting stay—And how they can finally break free.* MindBodyGreen. https://www.mindbodygreen.com/articles/why-victims-of-gaslighting-stay-and-how-to-finally-leave

Sarkis, S. A. (2019, July 12). *Rebuilding after a gaslighting or narcissistic relationship.* Psychology Today. https://www.psychologytoday.com/za/blog/here-there-and-everywhere/201907/rebuilding-after-gaslighting-or-narcissistic-relationship

Sarkis, S. (2021, March 12). *How to regain your sanity after you've been gaslighted.* MindBodyGreen. https://www.mindbodygreen.com/articles/what-to-do-when-youve-been-gaslighted

7 ways to control your thoughts. (n.d.). Tony Robbins. https://www.tonyrobbins.com/how-to-focus/how-to-control-your-mind/

Shull, M. (n.d.). *How to cope when you love a narcissist.* Mary Shull Counseling. https://www.maryshull.com/blog/how-to-cope-when-you-love-a-narcissist/#:~:text=It%20is%20a%20complicated%20mental

Smith, M., & Robinson, L. (2022, November 14). *Narcissistic personality disorder.* HelpGuide. https://www.helpguide.org/articles/mental-disorders/narcissistic-personality-disorder.htm

Stiefvater, S. (2022, March 10). *7 long-term effects of gaslighting (& how to recover).* PureWow. https://www.purewow.com/wellness/long-term-effects-of-gaslighting

Sweet, P. L. (2022). *How gaslighting manipulates reality.* Scientific American. https://www.scientificamerican.com/article/how-gaslighting-manipulates-reality/

Telloian, C. (2021, September 15). *5 types of narcissism and how to spot each.* Psych Central. https://psychcentral.com/health/types-of-narcissism

THC Editorial Team. (2022, January 15). *Emotional self-care: Importance, benefits, practices.* The Human Condition. https://thehumancondition.com/emotional-self-care-importance-benefits-practices/

Why are personal relationships important? (2021, December 16). Eugene Therapy. https://eugenetherapy.com/article/why-are-personal-relationships-important-3/#:~:text=through%20rough%20times.-

Wooll, M. (2022, January 27). *Learning the art of making mistakes.* BetterUp. https://www.betterup.com/blog/learning-from-your-mistakes

Printed in Great Britain
by Amazon

19637211R00102